Wainwrights without a Car
A Year on the Lake District Fells
Ron Kenyon

'It's not the destination, it's the journey.'

Ralph Waldo Emerson.

Publisher : Jagged Lakes Publications, Penrith
Text copyright © Ron Kenyon 2025

ISBN-978-1-3999-8168-2
A catalogue record for this book is available from the British Library.
All photographs are by the author unless otherwise stated.

"Wainwright bagging is all about a reason for adventure. Without a car you will find much more on each of the 214 outings. You'll interact with more interesting characters and unanticipated twists and turns will no doubt lead to a richer, deeper experience as well as a clearer environmental conscience. An exciting, original and environmental way to approach the classic Wainwrights."

Leo Houlding - *Cumbrian born Climber, Mountaineer and Adventurer of World Renown.*

"Ron Kenyon is a formidable walker and observer, with a deep affection, energy and empathy for Cumbria."

Rory Stewart - *British academic, broadcaster and former diplomat and politician.*

"Back in the day when Wainwright himself sought to climb all the fells, a bus could be counted on for almost every corner of Lakeland. Time and cuts have taken their toll making it a magnificent achievement to actually produce a book and a record to show how it can still be possible to claim your summits in the time-honoured way by public transport."

Mark Richards - *Inspired by walking with AW to develop his passion for pen drawing, he became an outdoor writer and a podcast presenter. www.Countrystride.co.uk podcast*

"This great book shows how we can do the Wainwrights as AW himself did by using public transport and encourages everyone to try new ways that have less impact on the environment."

Steve Birkinshaw - *An exceptional orienteer and fell runner who completed the Wainwrights in under a week in 2014.*

"Following the Wainwrights gives structure to seeing parts of the Lake District that perhaps you would not otherwise see. In seeing the fells guided by AW you can see how time has passed in the brilliant drawings in his books, but following these guides using local transport will really immerse you in the local culture and will add an extra sense of adventure to the journey. As a Mountain Rescue member I am often asked if most call outs are related to people in trainers etc, but in my experience most are experienced outdoors people who have been caught out, so whenever you go out ensure you have sufficient equipment and time, and let someone know what your plan is and what time you expect to be home.
Check out www.adventuresmart.uk"

Rob Hunter - *Chair (2024) - Penrith Mountain Rescue Team.*

We think this book would have AW's full approval. AW was not a great car fan and even when he was in a position financially to afford one it was never on his list of must-haves. When AW began writing his famous Pictorial Guides, he set out to complete them using public transport. The Society did discover, however, that he accepted lifts from a friend to the western Lakes as this area was, at the time, infrequently served by regular bus services. AW even admitted, in a letter, to completing Book Seven with "much shameful use of taxis".

AW came to appreciate the benefits of car ownership in his own life. Betty, his wife, drove AW to Wester Ross, Sutherland and other places. But it was quite different when he wrote about the adverse effects of car ownership on the upland landscapes he loved. He came to resent the post-war changes brought about by the exponential growth of motor cars. He was critical of policies which helped facilitate greater car use within the Lake District. In one of his books, he went so far as to suggest that motorists should be excluded from certain roads in the more secluded valleys. It could be said that AW had a love-hate relationship with the motor car. In later life he came to appreciate the freedom it gave him to explore areas he had never seen, but he could not quite forgive the damage he perceived to his beloved Lake District and other upland landscapes wrought by the proliferation of the motor car and the detrimental changes it brought in its wake.

If this book encourages more people to use public transport to access the fells, I'm sure AW would strongly recommend it to all who love the great beauty of the Lake District.

The Wainwright Society

Descending from Latrigg during the first walk of the EVMC Wainwright Challenge looking towards Blencathra, the Mell Fells and the Pennines (Walk **NF1**).

Maps are derived from Ordnance Survey OpenData TM

Every effort is made by the author to ensure the accuracy of this book as it goes to print. Changes occur over time - in particular with the timetables for buses and trains from year to year - and users should check with other sources of information, as referred to in the book. This book should be used as a reference book for planning walks and trips out in the Lake District together with maps, guidebooks and timetables for buses, trains and boats in the area.

Publisher :	Jagged Lakes Publications, Penrith
Website :	www.jaggedlakes.co.uk
Email :	info@jaggedlakes.co.uk
Facebook :	Wainwrights without a car - Jagged Lakes
Design :	Chris Sherwin - csdesigns
Maps :	Don Sargeant
Printed and Bound :	Bell and Bain Ltd., Glasgow
Distributor :	Cordee
	11 Jacknell Road,
	Dodwells Industrial Estate,
	Hinkley, LE10 3BS
	(t) 01455 61185
	(e) sales@cordee.co.uk
	(w) www.cordee.co.uk

CONTENTS

Testimonials

Prologue

Introduction	1
Getting to know the area	5
Valleys	11
Getting around the area	31
Accommodation	43
Have a plan and come back safely	47
Details and tales of the fells	49
Eastern Fells	51
Far Eastern Fells	71
Central Fells	87
Northern Fells	103
Southern Fells	115
North Western Fells	133
Western Fells	147
Other suggested routes	164
List of all Wainwrights - tick list	169
Best Views in the Lakes	174
Wainwright Rounds and Relays	180
Glossary	182
Fix the Fells	192
Eden Valley Mountaineering Club	198
Acknowledgements	199
General Index	201

INTRODUCTION

Alfred Wainwright (AW) produced his collection of pictorial guides to the Lake District fells in the 1950/60s and these books have encouraged many to venture onto the fells. What would he think of the Lake District now with the many millions visiting the area each year and the huge number of people going onto these fells - especially the honeypot summits such as Scafell Pike, Helvellyn, Skiddaw or Catbells?

The 1950s were a different time when car ownership was nothing like it is nowadays with so many now reliant on their cars for all their journeys. AW did not drive and many of his trips to the Lakeland fells, initially from Blackburn and then Kendal, were by bus. Needless to say this would have needed much planning though there were probably more buses in those days.

EVMC WAINWRIGHT CHALLENGE

The Eden Valley Mountaineering Club (EVMC) is based in Penrith, in the Eden Valley on the edge of the Lake District. Its members are involved in all aspects of rock climbing, walking and mountaineering. At the end of 2022, one of the members, Robin Illingworth, suggested at the AGM that we should take on the challenge of ascending all the Wainwrights, during 2023, without a car. This was to raise awareness of how using public transport can reduce our carbon footprint when pursuing outdoor activities. Admittedly there is quite a large carbon footprint associated with some members of the Club going off to various places around the world, but we thought that this challenge would help to focus minds to reduce car use and to make us think how we might travel more efficiently and sustainably.

We set off on this quest with the first summit, Latrigg, being climbed on a lovely day in January, with snow-covered fells around. With good access from Penrith to Keswick and the Ullswater area, interest was first focused on these regions. Details of the summits ascended were recorded on the EVMC website (www.evmc.co.uk) and details of the walks and ascents were added to the Facebook page - EVMC Wainwright Challenge.

The X4/X5 bus to Keswick became a regular mode of transport and we became familiar with the buses in the area. The use of the railway system as well as boats on the lakes were also drawn into the travel plans. A bike was used for one trip and could, no doubt, have been used elsewhere.

As we moved further away from Penrith, overnight accommodation became necessary for some of the trips with a wide variety of types of accommodation being available with hotels, climbing huts and camping.

Blencathra (or Saddleback) is one of the most accessible and popular summits from Penrith with fine views over the Lake District. We decided, early on, that it would be good to have a mass ascent of Blencathra as the final summit and, on 16th December, a number of members set off on the bus from Penrith, Blencathra bound, to complete the ascent of our 214th Wainwright without a car.

During the year I began to consider the idea of producing a book about ascending the Wainwrights without a car. This was mainly to promote the idea of leaving your vehicle at home or at your holiday accommodation and of using the buses, boats and trains to get around.

For many, the use of a car is not an option and, when one lives in a city or town, ownership of a car is not always necessary or just not practical. In London 46% of households do not own a car. It has been really interesting to learn about the public transport networks, both in the Lake District and elsewhere in the UK.

There is a cost in using public transport but this was helped in 2023 and also in 2024 with the charge of £2.00 per journey being available, though some of the EVMC members and other bus users, needless to say, have pensioner bus passes. The £2.00 bus charge has been a good way of encouraging bus use. It has been extended to December 2025, with a £3.00 maximum bus charge, and I hope this or something similar will be available in the future.

Using public transport opens up ideas of linear walks, in particular going from one valley to another, rather than circular walks returning to the starting points. This also removes the need to find a car parking place as well as not having the issue of traffic jams - although the bus driver still has that to contend with!

IS THIS A GUIDE OR A REFERENCE BOOK?

There are 214 Wainwrights with many ways to ascend them. Without a car one has to be more imaginative about how to access a particular fell and area. The main objective of this book is to highlight the transport systems available in the Lake District. This book is not a guidebook to climbing the Wainwrights, though details are given of the routes taken by the members of EVMC during 2023. Some of the routes are the obvious and the most common routes but others have been done to fit in with using a bus or other routes followed. There are also some rather quirky ways - the rock climb "Main Route to the Perch" on Hartsop above How comes to mind and this is definitely not recommended to walkers. Access to a particular area and which route one takes are dependent on where you start and what public transport is available.

I am a great advocate of using a paper map but there are also digital map devices available which are an amazing addition to the navigational armoury.

Use of a map not only assists you in knowing where you are and where you are going but is also invaluable in planning a trip out onto the fells. Then there are the various bus, train and boat time-tables with which to plan a day. Wainwright's guides or other similar guides, such as the Fellranger series, give invaluable insight and details of routes up the fells. It is hoped that this book will help draw together all of the above to aid you with your car-free adventures onto the Lakeland fells.

INTRODUCTION

HOW TO USE THIS BOOK

The following indicate the basis of terms and references used throughout the book.

- ▲ AW - Alfred Wainwright's initials are well-known and used instead of his full name.
- ▲ Fell - the Cumbrian name for hill or mountain is FELL - this derives from Norse or Viking name of *fjell* and has been used throughout the book.
- ▲ Transport information has been highlighted with symbols.
- ▲ Personal stories or comments have been included in italics.
- ▲ Summits which are Wainwrights have been highlighted in bold.
- ▲ Reference to details in the Glossary are highlighted in blue (page 182).
- ▲ Reference to 12 Best Views are highlighted in green (page 174).
- ▲ There are references throughout the book to the routes described in Chapter 7 under the various areas as follows -
  - o Northern Fells walk number 4 over Binsey - Walk **NF4**
  - o North Western Fells walk number 5 over Whinlatter - Walk **NWF5**
  - o Southern Fells walk number 3 over Lingmell - Walk **SF3**
- ▲ There are grid references included for various locations such as bus stops and fine views. These are indicated in brackets such as for the Stonethwaite bus stop in Borrowdale - (NY 257 142). QR codes and Longitudinal/Latitudinal references have not been used.

The website *www.jaggedlakes.co.uk* has been set up with additional information and links.

Corrections and updates to information in this book will be shown on the website.

Facebook page - *Wainwrights Without a Car - Jagged Lakes* - is for use by people to record trips out in the Lake District without the use of a car and also any comments about routes etc.
This book has been self published by Jagged Lakes Publications and is looking to donate one third of any income from the book to the organisation Fix the Fells (see page 192) with the bulk of the rest being given to other Cumbrian local causes and charities.
Since the end of 2023 I have not given up using my car though my perspective on the use of public transport and cutting down on the use of cars has decidedly changed. There are many occasions when time is not available or it is just not practical to leave the car but it is amazing what can be done if you leave those car keys at home or at your accommodation.
It is good to watch the world go by, especially from the front seat of a double-decker bus.
I hope this book will give you some new ideas and inspiration to use public transport to get around the Lake District, and elsewhere, and open up a new world away from the car...
and make you ponder on the quote attributed to American philosopher Ralph Waldo Emerson - 'It's not the destination, it's the journey'.

Ron Kenyon, January 2025

Above left: The Borrowdale 78 Bus Service - between Keswick and Seatoller at Rosthwaite.
Above right: Westward bound - looking out to sea on the Cumbrian Coast Line (Walk **SF2**).

Bottom: One of those magical moments - view from Red Screes over the clouds with the Scafell Group in the distance - on Christmas Day 2006 and the same day as the view on page 53 (Walk **EF9**).

GETTING TO KNOW THE AREA

When going to an area, especially for the first time, it is good to gather together information either on-line or at, say, a Tourist Information Centre, with the likes of maps, route information and guide-books to help to familiarise yourself with the area and to plan activities there.
That knowledge can also help from a safety point of view when in the area.
Many people have a specific objective - e.g. Scafell Pike or "That Hill above Wasdale".
They go to an area and have no idea what else there is and consultation of a map or guidebook can very much enhance their knowledge and experience.
In doing the "Wainwrights without a Car", it is necessary to view the area with new eyes and draw further information from the bus, train and boat timetables and link that to maps, guidebooks and other information to help plan routes on the fells.

It is well worth going into or contacting one of the Tourist Information Centres around the Lake District to top up your knowledge of the area.

Ambleside	Coniston	Grasmere	Kendal
Keswick	Penrith	Ullswater	Windermere (Bowness)
(Moot Hall)		(Glenridding)	Windermere (Railway Station)

www.lakedistrict.gov.uk - official website of the Lake District National Park.
www.visitlakedistrict.com - official tourism website for the region.

GETTING TO KNOW THE AREA

It is also worth consulting the **Adventure Smart UK** website *www.adventuresmart.uk* to help in various ways in the Lake District and beyond.

What is **AdventureSmart UK** about? Every day thousands of people set off for an adventure in the great outdoors. Some choose sports such as rock climbing or coasteering whilst others take a less extreme approach such as walking, cycling or simply playing on the beach with the family. The majority will have a fantastic time and will take home treasured memories; for a few, their day will be marred by discomfort, brushes with danger or accidents and some will have to be helped by rescue and emergency services. Many of these incidents could have been easily avoided; with a little preparation, everyone can help to ensure that their adventure becomes a treasured memory, not a nightmare.

Adventure Smart UK is not an organisation but is a campaign that is delivered by the many partner organisations that want people to enjoy the great outdoors safely.

The main issues to consider before going onto the fells are -

- **Am I confident I have the KNOWLEDGE AND SKILLS for the day?**
- **Do I know what the WEATHER will be like?**
- **Do I have the right GEAR?**

There is a wealth of information, both physical and digital, about the Lake District but I hope this chapter will help to focus thoughts and help you get to know the area and plan trips.

Navigation

Have you got a map and compass? This is a question which can be asked of people starting up a fell and sadly the answer is often NO! Furthermore, do they know how to use them? Some on the fells have no idea where they are, where they are going and often where they have been! They have a notion of climbing a particular honeypot summit but no feel or idea about the area. This unfortunately can also lead to the local Mountain Rescue Team being called out. Sometimes things happen which are unforeseen but for many incidents some pre-knowledge and planning would have helped enormously.

There is a very good and clever sketch by a rather young Rowan Atkinson impersonating the Rt. Hon. Sir Marcus Browning MP giving a speech which raises the topic of "Where are you going and do you have a map?" - Google the internet and have a listen!

A map is so fundamental for many outings and especially when going onto the fells.

A map for navigation can be a paper map or a digital map or device. It is suggested that all going onto the fells should have the following –

- Paper Map
- Compass
- Whistle
- Fully charged Digital Map or Device

GETTING TO KNOW THE AREA

It is well worth persevering with the ability to use a paper map and compass. There are courses available to learn map and compass skills.

For many now, logging onto Satnav in the car or GPS on the fells is the only known way.

These are fantastic and very useful systems especially around a town or city as well as in thick mist and at night on the fells.

There are the likes of OS Maps which is a map app downloadable to one's mobile phone and is being developed all the time. It is so comforting to get the mobile phone out, dial in and see the arrow zoom onto the place where you are. It is also useful to have the map of the whole of the UK, in your pocket, to look at with a few taps. A useful element, now embedded in OS Maps, is OS Locate - this, at the press of a button, gives a compass but also a precise Grid Reference number of where you are which could be of use if, sadly, you need to contact a Mountain Rescue Team – though it is better to avoid that situation with better planning.

Further mapping apps include Outdoor Active (replaced View Ranger), FatMap, Hiiker and Anquet. There are many others. These often provide pre-set routes and associated information. The small dot or symbol on your map showing your location and direction of travel makes life much easier, until your batteries go flat!

There are a lot of GPS systems available but this book is not going into detail other than recommending having a digital system - they are a great addition to other navigational aids, such as a paper map.

However there is the obvious disadvantage of loss of battery power. This is especially a problem with a mobile phone often being used for other purposes, in particular taking photographs, but more importantly for communication. AA batteries and device batteries are affected by cold temperatures, wear out and go flat with use and can be damaged/dropped (OK - maps can blow away too!). Consider carrying spare batteries and/or a power pack. If there is an emergency and a Mountain Rescue Team has to be called and they are looking for a signal from that mobile phone then loss of battery power is going to be a huge issue. Spare battery and solar generation are possibilities but reducing use of the mobile phone in the first place is best to retain that battery power. Setting your phone on Flight Mode helps in this respect. There is the added cost for paper maps but these are then available for future use. They can also be laid out on a table for an overview for planning routes and trips, together with other information, and so enhance and hopefully make for more interesting and safer trips.

If you need the services of Mountain Rescue, call 999 and ask for the Police. When they answer, tell them that you require the local Mountain Rescue Team. When the MR caller responds they will ask about location, if known, and any possible casualty injuries. They will look to find the phone's location by sending a link to the user and, if lost, directions may be given by controllers to walkers to help them navigate down to safety without calling out the full team.

It would be better not to have to call on the services of the Mountain Rescue Team - they are there to help you but remember that they are a voluntary service and you managing your safe return from a day on the fells is much more preferable to a call-out of the team.

GETTING TO KNOW THE AREA

Maps for the Lake District

There is a wide variety of paper maps now available for the Lake District.

Ordnance Survey
The Lake District is too large an area to be covered by one of the 1:25000 OL maps and in fact four maps are required for the whole of the area as follows –

North Western Lakes
+ OL4 - covers Keswick, Buttermere and Cockermouth

North Eastern Lakes
+ OL5 - covers Ullswater, Penrith, Mungrisdale, Caldbeck, Lazonby

South Western Lakes
+ OL6 - covers Coniston, Ulverston, Duddon Valley, Eskdale and Wasdale

South Eastern Lakes
+ OL7 - covers Windermere, Ambleside, Kendal, Milnthorpe, Silverdale

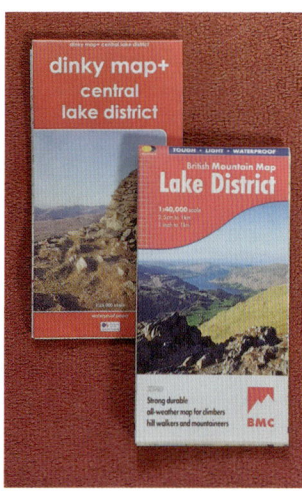

AZ Adventure Maps - Lake District
AZ produce maps for the whole of the UK including road maps. They produce a set of two maps, contained in booklet format, for the Northern and Southern Lake District.

Dinky Maps - Central Lake District
This map is based around the central area and overlaps the four OS area maps.

Harvey Maps
These maps were set up by Sue and Robin Harvey - Sue was UK orienteering champion with an interest in maps - and they have established a collection of maps, throughout the UK, linked with the outdoor enthusiast's world.

In collaboration with the British Mountaineering Council (BMC) Harvey Maps have produced a series of very detailed maps of the major outdoor areas around the UK. The scale for these maps is 1:40000 which is a slightly smaller scale than the Ordnance Survey Explorer maps. The Lake District map covers the central zone, similar to the Dinky (OS) Map mentioned here, but with the smaller scale it covers a larger area.

GETTING TO KNOW THE AREA

Harvey Maps also cover the Lake District with a collection of 1:25000 maps as follows –
- ▲ Lake District East
- ▲ Lake District North
- ▲ Lake District South East
- ▲ Lake District West

Guidebooks to the Lake District

There have been many guidebooks to the Lake District over the years since the 1700s giving details of all aspects of the area. There are few places in the world, if any, (New York City is the most written about city!) which have as many books written about them as the Lake District. There is such a wide range of Lake District themes which people write about (e.g. Wainwrights without a car!). There are many publications and lots of online information about walks in the Lake District.

To aid one in the quest to complete the "Wainwrights without a Car" and to give more ideas, then the following three publications give excellent detailed information about the various ways of ascending the Lake District fells.

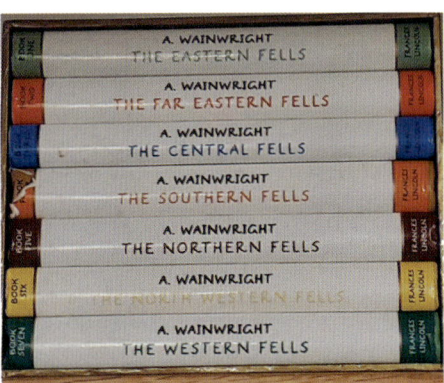

AW's Pictorial Guide to the Lake District

AW created his iconic series of very detailed guides in the 1950/60s and they have drawn many thousands to the fells over the years. He gave details of the various ways up the 214 summits (as well as the Outlying Fells) but also highlighted other aspects of the fells and shared his intimate knowledge with the readers and users of the guides. The guides have been updated but basically have the same well-used and popular format.

Fellranger Guides - Published by Cicerone

This is a very useful series of eight guides covering the Lake District written by Mark Richards who has an encyclopaedic knowledge of the Lake District fells. The guides contain Mark's own drawings of the fells, maps of the area and descriptions of the varied and many routes up the fells, and are illustrated by a fine selection of photographs. Overall, the guides give a comprehensive coverage over a wide area from Black Combe in the south to Binsey in the north and from Grike in the west to Grayrigg Forest, above the M6, in the east.

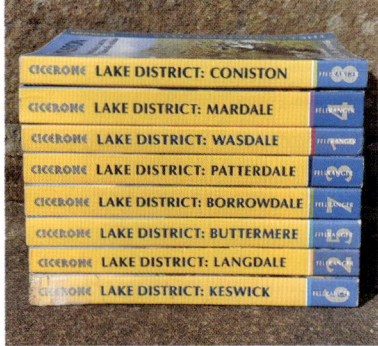

GETTING TO KNOW THE AREA

The Complete Lakeland Fells - by Bill Birkett

There are many more guides with a less comprehensive coverage. This guide contains all the Wainwrights (and more) but just in one volume.

Bill Birkett is a well-known Lakeland writer as well as rock climber who has lived in the Langdale area for all his life. He produced this book which documents 541 independent summits around the Lake District with suggested ascent routes. Bill has included all these summits as they all have something special about them. Collectively they are known as "The Birketts" and this is the Birketteer's Bible.

New versus old or make use of both! My wife and I were recently in Sheffield staying in a hotel near to the university, making use of the SATNAV and OS Maps but also had a 1970s Street Atlas. We were talking to a couple of young ladies, from Amsterdam, who were attending a conference on "Interaction of Computers and Humans". I mentioned the issue of the use of digital maps and needless to say she told me that she just uses digital maps and was not used to using a paper map. She had been in China where the use of digital maps is complicated by the fact that there is no access to Google (and Google Maps) and the local equivalent is all in Chinese. Digital maps are only one aspect of our "interaction" but as we "interact" more and more our dependency on the digital world increases and our knowledge of "the other world" can be reduced - no doubt this was discussed at the conference.

In contrast to this, in 2018 I was in Nepal helping the charity Juniper Trust (*www.junipertrust.org*) in the rebuilding of various schools following the earthquake there in 2015. As part of the trip we had been up the 4,000m peak called Pikey Peak to see the sunrise from the summit, with Everest and other Himalayan peaks in the distance. On the way down we stopped at a lodge for lunch (and a sleep). While there I was looking at my map of the area when three children came to have a look at what I was doing. Aged between 10 and 12, they attended the local school at Junbesi, a school established in the 1960s by Sir Edmund Hillary. This school was an hour and half walk down from there - and back uphill at the end of the day! They were most intrigued with the map and they spent a long time looking at it and pointing at and mentioning various locations around the area. I don't know if they had ever seen a map before but they soon appreciated what this map was and had an interesting time looking at it. I have a bee in my bonnet about using paper maps but can also see the benefits of using digital maps and feel that their combined use can enhance a visit to an area as well as aiding navigation and making a trip safer.

Young lads in Nepal, near Junbesi, showing much interest in a map of their area.

VALLEYS AROUND THE LAKE DISTRICT

The valleys of the Lake District are the key to accessing the area and the fells. They contain the towns and villages and with the roads and bus routes they link the area together.
This chapter looks at these valleys, what fells are close to them and, most importantly for this book, what public transport there is to that area.
Many thousands of years ago the area was a huge dome, with the highpoint at an equivalent of about 10,000 feet above what is now High Raise, near the Langdale Pikes. Over time, between 30,000 and 12,000 years ago, the area has experienced several glacial events, being covered in ice and glaciers, interspersed with warmer (interglacial) periods. The land was eroded and over time the valleys that we see today were created, like the spokes of a wheel, radiating from that central point. There was also a rift valley created from north to south, through earth movement, and this can be seen linking the valleys containing Bassenthwaite Lake, Thirlmere, Grasmere and Windermere. We are now left with the series of valleys, each with their own character, defining the landscape of the Lake District. There were moves, nearly 100 years ago, to create a road from Borrowdale to Wasdale over Styhead Pass but thankfully this was not done. There are various other roads which link valleys across the Lake District but 'when freed from the car' one is then able to traverse the fells and link up the valleys without the need for roads.

View of the Lake District from the pilot's seat at 30,000 feet - *photo Simon Curry*.

VALLEYS

This chapter gives details of the valleys and areas around the Lake District in a clockwise fashion starting from the Shap Fells area with Longsleddale. This contains:
▲ Details about each valley with towns and villages and surrounding fells.
▲ Details of the access by public transport and other means.

LONGSLEDDALE

This is the "long valley" reaching into the Far Eastern fells from the Kendal area.
There is no bus service up this valley and there is a feeling of remoteness here, even with a car. Consideration of camping overnight should be put into the planning.

 Access by bike up the valley, or from adjacent valleys, can give some interesting days out.

The upper section of Longsleddale with Kentmere Pike to the left (Walk **FEF6**).

VALLEYS

KENTMERE

Kentmere, like Longsleddale, reaches into the Far Eastern fells from the Kendal area and has the River Kent flowing through it which gave Kendal its name. There is also no bus service up the valley.

 Use of a bike here should be considered with access up the delightful valley from Staveley.

 There is the railway station at Staveley (SD 468 982) on the branch line between Oxenholme and Windermere.

 The 508 bus service travels between Windermere and Penrith, during March to November; this can be taken to Limefitt Park (NY 414 030) from where the Garburn Pass goes over to Kentmere. This bus service can also be considered for links at Kirkstone Pass (NY 401 080) and Hartsop (NY 405 131).

 There are a number of bus services which travel between Kendal and Windermere, which pass through Staveley at the bottom end of the Kentmere Valley but quite some way from the head of the valley.

The upper section of Kentmere from Shipman Knotts with Yoke, Ill Bell, Froswick and Thornthwaite Crag in the distance and a farmer, on his quad-bike, in the foreground (Walk **FEF6**).

VALLEYS
WINDERMERE

This is England's largest lake and many pass this way en route into the Lake District. The town of **Windermere** is set well above the lake, by the railway line, and just north of **Bowness-on-Windermere**, which is beside Windermere.

 Windermere Railway Station (SD 414 986) is at the end of the branch line from Oxenholme, which is one of the two mainline stations servicing the Lake District. It is quite a gathering point with people from many nations going through there, highlighted by the notice board in the languages of English, Chinese and Japanese.

 Windermere Railway Station is also a hub for buses to and from various locations as follows -

 Services throughout the year
- o 6 bus service -   Barrow, Ulverston, Windermere
- o 505 bus service -   Kendal, Windermere, Ambleside, Coniston
- o 516 bus service -   Kendal, Windermere, Ambleside, Elterwater, Dungeon Ghyll (Great Langdale)
- o 555 bus service -   Lancaster, Kendal, Windermere, Ambleside, Keswick
- o 599 bus service -   Bowness, Windermere, Ambleside, Grasmere
- o 755 bus service -   Morecambe, Carnforth, Windermere, Bowness

 Restricted service between March and November
- o 508 bus service -   Penrith, Ullswater, Patterdale, Windermere

 Windermere also has its own transport system with the Windermere Lake Cruises - *https://www.windermere-lakecruises.co.uk* - sailing up and down the lake, from Bowness-on-Windermere (SD 401 967), giving access to various locations along the lake including Waterhead at Ambleside (NY 377 031).

Near Windermere Railway Station (SD 414 986) is Orrest Head, which was AW's first Lakeland summit and is a fine viewpoint looking into the Lake District. If you have a few hours to spare then it is well worth ascending.

Ambleside is at the head of Windermere with the fells overlooking it and roads leading northward to Grasmere and Keswick and westwards to Langdale and Coniston. There is a lot of accommodation in the area along with many shops and hostelries. A visit to the Armitt Museum is well worth making to find out more about the area and its history.

VALLEYS

 There is the main bus stop on Kelsick Road (NY 376 042), in the centre of Ambleside, which is a busy hub for the various buses, mentioned above.

 Waterhead (NY 377 032) to the south of Ambleside, beside the lake, is the location to catch the Windermere Steamer.

599 bus service at Bowness-on-Windermere - *photo Stagecoach.*

GRASMERE AND RYDAL WATER

This is the area at the top end of the Windermere valley, made famous by its links back to William Wordsworth and friends. Encircled by fells, the popular Fairfield Horseshoe gives a good challenge on the north of the area and, to the west, Easedale and its tarn lead into the **High Raise** area and the likes of **Silver How**, **Blea Rigg** and **Helm Crag** nearer by. The ever popular **Loughrigg Fell** overlooks Rydal Water.

 The area is well serviced by buses:
    555 bus service -   Lancaster, Kendal, Windermere, Ambleside, Keswick.
    599 bus service -   Windermere, Ambleside, Grasmere.

VALLEYS
GREAT LANGDALE

This is the main valley of the Langdale area with Little Langdale to the south. At its head there are various routes which lead on into other valleys:

- ▲ Stake Pass goes over into Langstrath and Borrowdale.
- ▲ Rossett Gill leads on to Esk Hause and Wasdale or Borrowdale as well as to the Ennerdale and Buttermere valleys.
- ▲ The Band leads to Three Tarns and into Eskdale.

The iconic Langdale Pikes, with **High Raise** behind, form a very distinctive feature of the valley and can be seen from many locations including the M6 motorway.
Scafell Pike and nearby summits make a popular long day out going by Rossett Gill and Esk Hause - but remember the obvious saying - "Once you get there you have to come back!".
On the other side of the valley **Pike O'Blisco**, **Crinkle Crags** and **Bowfell** form a fine collection of summits with the lower **Lingmoor** to their east, above Blea Tarn.

As well as a number of hotels and similar accommodation in the valley there is the National Trust campsite, near Old Dungeon Ghyll (NY 286 060), as well as the Baysbrown Campsite, near Chapel Stile - (NY 315 053). There are also a number of climbing huts in the valley.

Great Langdale is served, all year, by the 516 bus service between Windermere Railway Station (SD 414 986), Ambleside (Kelsick Road) (NY 376 042) and Old Dungeon Ghyll (NY 286 060).

Great Langdale and beyond as seen from Crinkle Crags (Walk **SF4**).

VALLEYS

CONISTON

Coniston Water and the village of Coniston are at the southern end of the Lake District and are overlooked by **Coniston Old Man** and **Wetherlam**, encircling the Coniston Coppermines Valley to the West.

Just to the south of **Coniston Old Man** is **Dow Crag** and its impressive crags - a major rock climbing venue.

Just to the north, the rather lower fells of **Black Crag** and **Holme Fell** give fine views of their larger neighbours.

The village of Coniston is a busy place with a good selection of accommodation, campsites, shops and hostelries. A visit to the Ruskin Museum is well worth making to find out more about the area and its history.

   The 505 bus service travels between Windermere Railway Station (SD 414 986), Ambleside (Kelsick Road - NY 376 042) and Coniston (SD 302 975). This bus service also passes through Hawkshead (SD 353 980) and close to **Black Crag**.

   The Blueworks Bus Service - *https://www.blueworks.uk.com* travels from Barrow, via Ulverston, to Coniston.

   The Coniston Launches *https://conistonlaunch.co.uk/jetties* as well as the Gondola *https://www.nationaltrust.org.uk/visit/lake-district/steam-yacht-gondola* sail up and down Coniston Water and can give access to various locations around the lake, in particular on the east side of the lake at Brantwood, home of John Ruskin.

Blind Tarn and Brown Pike, near Dow Crag (Walk **SF6**).

18

VALLEYS

DUDDON VALLEY

This is a delightful valley with the Coniston area fells to the east and **Harter Fell** to the west. There is accommodation at places along the valley as well as a fine campsite at Turner Hall Farm GR (SD 232 963).

 There is a railway station at Foxfield on the Cumbria Coast Railway Line. This is at the south end of the valley, near Broughton-in-Furness, however there is no bus service in the valley.

 One can consider use of a bicycle or taxi to access the valley or it can be approached from the Coniston area over the Walna Scar Pass.

Duddon Valley with Wallowbarrow Crag on the left and Great Carrs in the distance.

ESKDALE

This is another delightful area and here you are usually well away from the crowds. Starting near Ravenglass area, by the sea, the Eskdale valley goes all the way to Esk Hause in the very centre of the Lake District.
To its east, **Green Crag**, **Harter Fell** and **Hard Knott** give a good walk whilst further up the valley are **Scafell** and **Scafell Pike** with **Bowfell** and **Crinkle Crags** across the valley. Just to the north of the main valley is Miterdale which can give access to **Whin Rigg** and **Illgill Head**. The pass from Boot over by Burnmoor Tarn can be used to access Wasdale Head as well as the fells around there. There is hotel accommodation and hostels along the valley as well as campsites.

VALLEYS

Looking down Eskdale from Hard Knott Pass (Walk **SF2**).

 Ravenglass (SD 085 964) is on the Cumbria Coast Railway Line.

 The main way of accessing the valley, without a car, is with La'al Ratty - the Ravenglass and Eskdale Railway - *https://ravenglass-railway.co.uk*. This is the iconic miniature railway which is based at the station at Ravenglass. There are a number of stations along the route of La'al Ratty.
- o Irton Road station (NY 148 005), near Eskdale Green, gives access to Miterdale which leads up to **Whin Rigg** and **Illgill Head**.
- o Dalegarth (NY 173 007) is the final station for La'al Ratty, in the hamlet of Boot, and gives access to the fells around there and beyond.

WASDALE

The valley with the Deepest Lake, the Highest Mountain, the Smallest Church and the Biggest Liar. This reaches right into the Lake District with dramatic mountains surrounding Wasdale Head with **Scafell**, **Scafell Pike**, **Great End**, **Great Gable**, **Kirk Fell** and **Pillar**.
Many only visit the valley with one purpose and that is the climbing of the highest mountain in England - **Scafell Pike**. This means that the path up there can be somewhat busy.
Sadly this also contributes to making the local Wasdale Mountain Rescue Team one of the busiest in the UK - so take care …. and there is much more to Wasdale than **Scafell Pike**!
At Wasdale Head there is accommodation, including the original home of British rock climbing at the Wasdale Head Inn, as well as the Barn Door climbing shop and the campsites at Wasdale Head. There are also accommodation and campsites, at the start of the valley, around Nether Wasdale.

VALLEYS

 During the summer, for the last few years, there has been the Wasdale Shuttle Bus which travels up and down the valley between Nether Wasdale and Wasdale Head. This has been run using local bus companies and it is hoped, with funding available, it will continue into the future. At the start and finish of each day there is a service linking to Ravenglass Station, which is useful to reach the Cumbrian Coast Railway Line.

See website - *www.lakedistrict.gov.uk/wasdaleshuttle*

 Alternatively there is access over the passes and fells from adjoining valleys as follows -

- From Eskdale   by Burnmoor Tarn
- From Langdale   by Rossett Gill, Esk Hause and Styhead Pass
- From Borrowdale   by Styhead Pass

Evening time in Wasdale.

Ennerdale from the High Level Route along to Pillar Rock, with Great Gable in the distance.

ENNERDALE

This is the long valley with the ridge of **Pillar** and **Haycock** to the south and **Great Borne**, **Red Pike** and **High Stile** to the north. The Ennerdale Horseshoe is a classic long walk and also a fell race.

There is accommodation at the Low Gillerthwaite Field Centre (NY 138 142) and also at Ennerdale YHA (NY 143 142) part way up the valley, beyond Ennerdale Water. Near the head of the valley is the iconic Black Sail Youth Hostel (NY 195 123) which is set in an amazing location.

 The nearest bus service is from Whitehaven, on the Cumbrian Coast Railway Line; this goes to Cleator Moor (NY 027 144) and Frizington (NY 033 169).

 There is a track along the length of the valley which is popular for mountain biking and use of a mountain bike could be considered in planning trips to this area.

VALLEYS

BUTTERMERE AND LOWESWATER

This valley contains the lakes of Buttermere and Crummock Water with Loweswater nearby. To the south of Buttermere and Crummock Water is the fine ridge starting with **Great Borne** and going over **Red Pike** and **High Stile** and on to AW's favourite fell of **Haystacks** before curving round to **Fleetwith Pike**.
Honister Pass links the valley to the Borrowdale valley and to its north is the ridge containing **Dale Head**, **Hindscarth** and **Robinson**.
The north side of Crummock Water is dominated by the bulks of **Whiteside** and **Grasmoor** then the diminutive **Rannerdale Knotts** leading to **Whiteless Pike** and **Wandope** and on up to **Eel Crag**.
In the area between Lorton and Loweswater are the often forgotten fells of **Low Fell** and **Fellbarrow**. Between Loweswater and Ennerdale is a collection of fells with its central summit of **Blake Fell** with ridges dropping away from it. These summits enjoy views out to the Solway Firth and Scotland as well as into the Lake District. Just to the south of Crummock Water, **Mellbreak** looms over the lake and Kirkstile Inn.

   Between March and November the 77 bus service follows a loop starting in Keswick, over Whinlatter Pass, to Lorton (NY 153 257), then up the valley by Lanthwaite Green (NY 158 208), Buttermere Village (NY 174 169) and Gatesgarth Farm (NY 194 149) then over Honister Pass (NY 225 135) to Borrowdale and back to Keswick.

   The 77A bus service does this loop in reverse.

   During the summer there is the 77C Buttermere Shuttle Bus service which runs between Cockermouth and Buttermere Village (NY 174 169).

View from Watching Crag, on Low Fell, to Crummock Water and beyond (Walk **WF5**).

NEWLANDS VALLEY

This is a side valley of Borrowdale with the **Catbells** to **High Spy** ridge to the east and **Barrow** and **Causey Pike** ridges to the west. At the head of the valley is the **Dale Head** to **Robinson** ridge dropping down to **Ard Crags** and **Knott Rigg**. Newlands Pass links Newlands Valley with the Buttermere valley, over the col, between **Robinson** and **Knott Rigg**.

The X5 bus service, between Penrith and Workington, passes through Braithwaite (NY 231 236) which is at the lower end of the valley and can be used to access the valley.

Between March and November the 77 / 77A bus services also pass through Braithwaite (NY 231 236) as well as by Hawse End (NY 247 212) below **Catbells** and can also be used to access the valley.

The Derwentwater Launches stop near Hawse End (NY 247 212) as well at other locations around Derwentwater.

Gary Newman at The Swineside Inn with Causey Pike beyond (Walk **NWF6**).

24

VALLEYS

BORROWDALE AND KESWICK

This is the valley which goes south from Keswick into the central fells of the Lake District and gives access to a wide area.
From the head of the valley, around Seatoller and Seathwaite, **Great End** and **Great Gable** command the view up the valley, with **Scafell Pike** hidden beyond. The major link route of Styhead Pass takes one from Seatoller over to Wasdale Head.
The ridge of **Glaramara** and **Allen Crags** stretches south to the central Lake District pass of Esk Hause.
Langstrath (a well-named long valley) branches off the main valley, through Stonethwaite and over Sticks Pass to Great Langdale. To its east, the ridge from **High Raise** goes northwards over **Ullscarf**, **High Seat** and **Bleaberry Fell** before dropping down to Keswick.
On the west side of the valley, the ridge from **High Spy** goes over **Maiden Moor** and the extremely popular **Catbells**. This is best approached from the south, with a fine view from **Maiden Moor** of **Catbells** with Keswick and **Skiddaw** behind.

Reflections in Derwentwater around the sculpture near Friar's Crag.

VALLEYS

To the north of Keswick, **Skiddaw** and its neighbouring summits tower above the town and, being one of the main four 3,000 foot summits in the Lake District, **Skiddaw** is a popular challenge. There is a lot of accommodation and several campsites in the Keswick area together with shops and hostelries. A visit to the Keswick Museum is well worth making to find out more about the area and its history.

Keswick is one of the main towns in the Lake District and is a major transport hub with a very busy bus station with buses passing through as follows –

Services throughout the year -

- 78 bus service -   Keswick, Borrowdale, Seatoller
- 554 bus service -   Carlisle, Wigton, Keswick
- 555 bus service -   Keswick, Ambleside, Windermere, Kendal, Lancaster
- X4 bus service -   Penrith, Threlkeld, Keswick, east side of Bassenthwaite Lake, Castle Inn, Embleton, Cockermouth, Workington
- X5 bus service -   Penrith, Threlkeld, Keswick, Braithwaite, west side of Bassenthwaite Lake, Embleton, Cockermouth, Workington

Restricted services - between March and November

- 77 bus service -   Daily - Keswick, Whinlatter, Buttermere, Seatoller, Catbells, Keswick
- 77A bus service -   as 77 bus service but in reverse
- 509 bus service -   Saturdays, Sundays and Bank Holidays only - Keswick, Patterdale, Pooley Bridge, Lowther Castle, Penrith
- 553 bus service -   Saturdays, Sundays and Bank Holidays only - Carlisle, Dalston, Caldbeck, Uldale, Keswick

On Derwentwater, the Derwentwater Launches - *https://keswick-launch.co.uk* are based at Keswick and sail around the lake stopping at a number of piers. There are stops at Hawse End (NY 247 212) and High Brandlehow (NY 252 197), which are useful for the **Catbells** ridge, and stops at Lodore (NY 263 188) and Ashness (NY 268 203), which are useful for the **High Seat** ridge.

Borrowdale bound on the top deck of the 78 bus service (Walk **CF8**).

THIRLMERE

Thirlmere was established in the 1880s as a water supply for the growing city of Manchester. It is situated in the Lake District's own rift valley going from north to south across the spokes of the "valley wheel". The main A591 goes through the valley and can be accessed from the north from the Keswick area and from the south, over Dunmail Raise, from Ambleside and Grasmere.

It is dominated on its east by the Helvellyn Range which stretches from **Clough Head**, just south of Threlkeld, to **Dollywaggon Pike**, overlooking Dunmail Raise. **Helvellyn** is one of the four main 3,000 foot summits in the Lake District and is justly popular. To the west the broad ridge from **High Raise** northwards goes over **Ullscarf, High Seat** and **Bleaberry Fell** before dropping into Keswick.

 The 555 bus service travels between Lancaster and Keswick via Kendal, Windermere, Ambleside and Grasmere.

 There are useful bus stops at -
- Stanah (NY 317 189) at the foot of Sticks Pass providing access to Glenridding and fells to the north.
- Swirls Car Park (NY 315 170) at the start of one of the main paths up **Helvellyn**.
- Wythburn (NY 324 136) at the start of another path up **Helvellyn**.
- The top of Dunmail Raise (NY 326 117) giving an elevated start to routes in the area.

 Thirlmere restricts access westwards but there are useful bus stops at -
- Steel End (NY 322 128) in Wythburn Valley, at the south end of Thirlmere.
- Bridge End (NY 315 194) near the dam at the north end of Thirlmere.
- Shoulthwaite (NY 300 205) for the Shoulthwaite valley.

VALLEYS

THE SKIDDAW RANGE

The most northerly area of the Lake District contains the Skiddaw Range, named after the highest summit in that area. Just to its east is **Blencathra** which presents an impressive façade overlooking the village of Threlkeld and the A66 road between Penrith and Keswick. **Blencathra** is also known as Saddleback with the pronounced saddle between its twin summits. The area to the north is somewhat cut off from general view and is known as Bac'o'Skidda or Back of Skiddaw. The main rock type of this area is Skiddaw Slate which is a much softer rock than that around other areas in the Lake District and the fells here are much more rounded and less dramatic than elsewhere.

These more northerly fells are difficult to access by bus.
- The X4/X5 bus services travel between Penrith and Workington, via Threlkeld and Keswick, with the X4 going along the east side of Bassenthwaite Lake and beside **Dodd** and **Ullock Pike**.
- The 554 bus service travels between Carlisle and Keswick, going along the east side of Bassenthwaite Lake, by **Dodd**, as well as near the village of Bassenthwaite and the fell of **Binsey** beyond.
- On Saturdays, Sundays and Bank Holidays, between March and November, the 553 bus service travels between Carlisle and Keswick via Caldbeck, Uldale and Bassenthwaite.
Though somewhat limited, this service gives useful access to the north side of the Lake District.

A bike would be useful to access this area.

View from Lonscale Fell to Skiddaw House with Great Calva and Knott beyond (Walk **NF7**).

VALLEYS

ULLSWATER

On the north-east side of the Lake District, this is a very popular valley encircled by many summits. To the west is the Helvellyn Ridge stretching from Kirkstone Pass, over **Fairfield** and **Helvellyn** to **Clough Head**.

To the south is the High Street ridge with the smaller outliers of **Place Fell** and **Hallin Fell**. There is the potential of a very long horseshoe, along the watershed of the valley, from Threlkeld along the Helvellyn Ridge to Kirkstone Pass, then across to **High Street** and along the ridge northwards to Heughscar and down to Pooley Bridge.

The 508 bus service travels between Penrith and Windermere between March and November and between Penrith and Patterdale during the winter months.

On Saturdays, Sundays and Bank Holidays, between March and November, the 509 bus service travels between Keswick and Penrith, via Patterdale, Pooley Bridge and Lowther Castle. This is well worth considering for facilitating access from Keswick to, say, Glenridding before walking back over **Helvellyn** to Thirlmere to catch the 555 bus service back into Keswick.

The Ullswater Hopper bus service is a recent summer-only service, useful to access places around the valley. Details are in "The Lakes by Bus" booklet and website - https://situcumbria.org.uk/ullswater-bus

The Ullswater Steamers is the steamer service which sails up and down Ullswater calling at Glenridding, Aira Force, Howtown and Pooley Bridge en route - https://www.ullswater-steamers.co.uk

PENRITH

Penrith is located on the east side of the Lake District on the West Coast Main Railway Line as well as the M6. It is close to the Settle to Carlisle Railway Line which runs between Yorkshire and Carlisle and has stations, in the Eden Valley, at Appleby and Langwathby. Penrith is the main town in the Eden Valley, an area which has been described, from a visitors' point of view, as Cumbria's Best Kept Secret. The town is near the River Eamont and River Lowther, which flow out of the Ullswater and the Haweswater areas. There is the newly established Eamont Way footpath, which goes from the railway station to Pooley Bridge and links to the Ullswater Way - https://www.ullswaterheritage.org. The A66 road is the main link road across the country from Scotch Corner, in the east, by Penrith to Keswick and beyond.

There are the following bus services in the area -
- o   X4/X5 bus service - Penrith to Workington via Threlkeld and Keswick.
- o   508 bus service - Penrith to Windermere (March to November) - just to Patterdale in the winter.
- o   104 bus service - between Centre Parcs (Whinfell) and Carlisle.
- o   509 bus service - Penrith to Keswick on Saturdays, Sundays and Bank Holidays (March to November) via Lowther Castle, Pooley Bridge and Patterdale.

Various Fellrunner bus services - *http://www.fellrunnerbus.co.uk*
- o   Including 111 bus service - Penrith to Burnbanks (Haweswater) on Thursdays.

Haweswater with the Eden Valley and Pennines beyond, from Mardale III Bell (Walk **FEF6**).

MARDALE (HAWESWATER)

This valley is on the eastern side of the Lake District and contains the reservoir of Haweswater which was established by the Manchester Corporation in the 1930s. At the head of the valley are the fells of the High Street Ridge and fells extending northwards, to the west of the valley. To its east, **Harter Fell** towers menacingly above the head of the lake with **Selside Pike** and **Branstree** nearby.

 There is the Haweswater Hotel which is part way along the valley and could be considered as accommodation for the area.

 The Fellrunner Bus services - *http://www.fellrunnerbus.co.uk*
This is a very important transport system around the Eden Valley giving links from the villages and hamlets of the area to the likes of Penrith. On a Thursday there is the 111 bus service from Penrith to Burnbanks, below the dam for Haweswater, and this gives an interesting access to this area.

 A bicycle would be useful to access the valley and the fells around it.

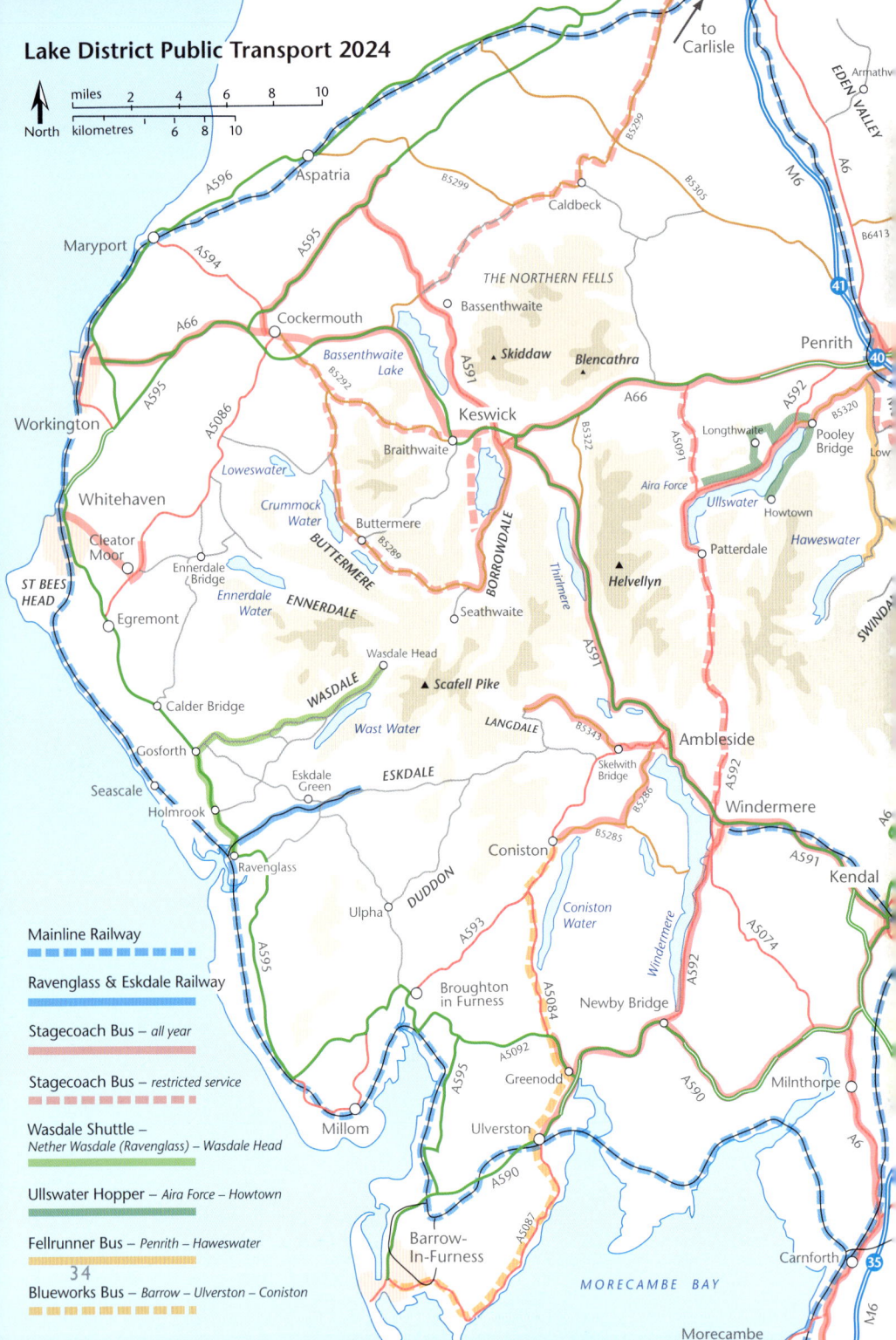

GETTING AROUND THE AREA

Langdale bound on the 516 bus service (Walk **SF4**).

This chapter looks at the various ways of travelling around the area without the use of a car including buses, trains, steamers and launches as well as bicycles and shanks' pony.

RAILWAYS

The main **West Coast Main Railway Line** travels up the west side of the United Kingdom from London to Glasgow with access to the Lake District at:-

The Windermere train arriving at Oxenholme Station.

Oxenholme and the Lake District: this is located near Kendal and from here a branch line goes by Kendal and Staveley to Windermere. Originally there were plans to take the railway further into the Lake District to Grasmere but there was great opposition and the line stopped at Windermere, from where a comprehensive selection of bus services leads into the Lake District. The name of the station should be Oxenholme and the South Lakes to help avoid confusion with passengers getting off here to go to, for example, Keswick and the North Lakes. The travel time, by rail, from London to Oxenholme is just under three hours.

Penrith and the North Lakes: there is a good transport hub at the railway station here with bus services going to Keswick as well as to the Ullswater valley. Penrith itself is an important hub for this area, servicing the Eden Valley and the north-east section of the Lake District. There used to be a railway from Penrith, via Keswick, to Workington but this was closed in the 1970s. There have been moves to reopen it but, with the establishment of the footpath and cycleway between Keswick and Threlkeld, and the ever-increasing cost, the chance of it reopening is diminishing - but who knows? The travel time, by rail, from London to Penrith is just over three hours.

GETTING AROUND THE AREA

The Cumbrian Coast Railway Line follows the Cumbrian coast after it branches off the West Coast Main Line at Lancaster, by Carnforth, and goes along through Barrow, Millom, Ravenglass, Whitehaven and Workington before rejoining the Main Line at Carlisle. This provides a useful way of getting into West Cumbria to the likes of Ravenglass, Whitehaven and Workington before using other means to get into the Lake District. Currently the area is serviced by the Avanti and Northern Rail franchises and details of journeys can be found on Trainline *(https://www.trainline)* or at Ticket Offices at stations.

The Settle - Carlisle Railway Line runs through the Eden Valley, to the east of the Lake District. This links West Yorkshire and the Yorkshire Dales to the Eden Valley and Carlisle. There are stations, along the way, at Appleby and Langwathby from which there are some bus services or one could consider a taxi or use a bike to go to Penrith.

The Ravenglass and Eskdale Railway is located in the Eskdale Valley and is also known as La'al Ratty. This is a miniature railway which was originally established for the extraction of quarried rock but was converted into a passenger train and steams up and down the valley from Ravenglass, on the Cumbrian Coast Railway line. It initially goes through Miterdale then Eskdale to Dalegarth, which is well up the Lower Eskdale valley and ideal for access to the fells around there and beyond. Further details about La'al Ratty and the timetable for trains are available on the website - *https://ravenglass-railway.co.uk*

La'al Ratty (River Mite) at Ravenglass.

BUSES

77A Bus at the summit of Honister Pass.

 ## Stagecoach

The main bus services for the area are run by Stagecoach which has a comprehensive timetable across much of Cumbria and the Lake District.

The bus timetables change from year to year and the following details are based on the timetable from March to November 2024 with details of changes for 2025 obtained in January 2025. Some services are not available during the winter and some operate just on Saturdays, Sundays and Bank Holidays, and you should consult up to date timetables.

The bus timetable is online (*https://www.stagecoach.com*) and there is a very useful booklet available at various locations including Tourist Information Centres and bus stations.

The following services can be of use in your quest to climb the Wainwrights without a car.

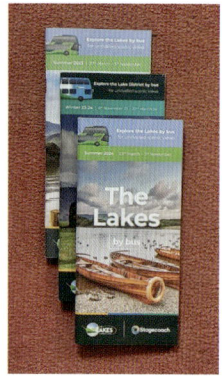

Bus Timetables of Stagecoach for 2023 and 2024.

GETTING AROUND THE AREA

- 6 bus service — Barrow, via Ulverston to Windermere
- 30 bus service — Whitehaven to Frizington, via Cleator Moor
- 78 bus service — Keswick to Seatoller (Borrowdale Valley)
- 505 bus service — Windermere to Coniston via Ambleside and Hawkshead
- 516 bus service — Windermere to Dungeon Ghyll (Great Langdale) via Ambleside
- 554 bus service — Carlisle to Keswick via Wigton and Bothel
- 555 bus service — Keswick to Lancaster via Grasmere, Ambleside, Windermere and Kendal
- 599 bus service — Bowness-on-Windermere to Grasmere via Ambleside
- 600 bus service — Carlisle to Cockermouth via Wigton and Bothel
- 755 bus service — Bowness-on-Windermere to Morecambe via Kendal and Carnforth
- X4 bus service — Penrith to Workington via Keswick and Bassenthwaite (on the east side of Bassenthwaite Lake)
- X5 bus service — Penrith to Workington via Keswick, Braithwaite and Thornthwaite (on the west side of Bassenthwaite Lake)
- 77 bus service — Keswick to Buttermere, via Whinlatter, then over Honister Pass and back, by Grange and Catbells to Keswick
- 77A bus service — As 77 but in reverse
- 77C bus service — Cockermouth to Buttermere
- 508 bus service — Penrith to Windermere, via Pooley Bridge, Glenridding and Patterdale - this service operates during the period from March to November but just goes between Penrith and Patterdale during the winter months

Services on Saturdays, Sundays and Bank Holidays between March and November

- 509 bus service — Keswick to Penrith, via Dockray, Patterdale, Pooley Bridge and Lowther Castle
- 553 bus service — Carlisle to Keswick via Caldbeck and Uldale

OTHER BUS SERVICES

There are nationwide bus services with **National Express** (*www.nationalexpress.com*), stopping at Penrith and Carlisle, and **Megabus** (*www.megabus.co.uk*), stopping at Carlisle.

There are various other bus services around the Lake District which are dependent on funding and demand. These provide an important travel link for the local residents as well as a useful service for visitors to the area and all additional use will help to maintain them.

GETTING AROUND THE AREA

 Blueworks

Blueworks provides rural transport with bus and taxi services for the South Lakeland and Furness Peninsula. In particular, it provides a bus service between Barrow and Coniston, via Ulverston. Further details are available on the website - *https://www.blueworks.uk.com*

Blueworks Bus at Coniston.

Wasdale Shuttle Bus.

 Wasdale Shuttle Bus

During the summer, for the last few years, there has been the Wasdale Shuttle Bus which travels up and down the valley of Wasdale, between Nether Wasdale and Wasdale Head. This has been run using local bus companies and it is hoped that, with funding available, it will continue operating into the future. At the start and finish of each day there is a service linking to Ravenglass Station, which is useful to reach the Cumbrian Coast Railway Line.
See website - *www.lakedistrict.gov.uk/wasdaleshuttle*

GETTING AROUND THE AREA

 ## Ullswater Hopper

The Ullswater Hopper (UB1) bus service is a recently introduced service, operating during the summer, which has been developed to help with transport along the Ullswater valley linking Aira Force, Watermillock, Pooley Bridge and Howtown. It is operated by Stagecoach and details are in "The Lakes by Bus" booklet and website: *https://situcumbria.org.uk/ullswater-bus*

Ullswater Hopper bus at The Quiet Site with Little Mell Fell behind.

 ## The Fellrunner Bus services

This is a very important transport system around the Eden Valley giving links between the villages and hamlets of the area and the towns. Details of routes are available on the website - *http://www.fellrunnerbus.co.uk*

Fellrunner buses in Penrith.

38

GETTING AROUND THE AREA

 **BOATS AND STEAMERS ON THE LAKES**

The Lake District is famous for its lakes and a number of these have boats, steamers or launches operating on them for the public. These go to locations around the lakes and can be a useful and pleasant way of travelling.

Windermere Lake Cruises

Windermere has its own transport system - Windermere Lake Cruises. This can be joined at various locations such as -

- Bowness-on-Windermere (SD 401 967)
- Waterhead at Ambleside (NY 377 031)
- Lakeside (SD 378873), at the south end
- Brockhole (NY387 012)
- Wray Castle (NY 376 013)

More details are on the website - *https://www.windermere-lakecruises.co.uk*

Windermere Steamer.

GETTING AROUND THE AREA

 Coniston Launches and The Gondola

The Coniston Launches, as well as the steam-powered Gondola, cruise around Coniston Water give access to various locations, in particular on the east side of the lake.
Further details on the websites -

   Coniston Launches
    https://conistonlaunch.co.uk/jetties
   The Steam Yacht Gondola
    https://www.nationaltrust.org.uk/visit/lake-district/steam-yacht-gondola

Coniston Gondola.

40

GETTING AROUND THE AREA

 ## Derwentwater Launches

The Derwentwater Launches are based at Keswick and cruise around the lake, stopping at a number of piers, in both clockwise and anticlockwise directions.
There are in particular stops at –

- Hawse End (NY 247 212) and High Brandlehow (NY 252 197), which are useful for the **Catbells** ridge on the west side of Borrowdale valley
- Lodore (NY 263 188) and Ashness (NY 268 203), which are useful for the **High Seat** ridge on the east side of the Borrowdale valley

More details are available on the website - *https://keswick-launch.co.uk*

 ## The Ullswater Steamers

This is the steamer service which cruises up and down Ullswater calling at -
- Glenridding (NY 390 170)
- Aira Force (NY400 1968)
- Howtown (NY 443 199)
- Pooley Bridge (NY 467 243)

More details are available on the website - *https://www.ullswater-steamers.co.uk*

Steamer on Ullswater with Caudale Moor and Arnison Crag beyond.

GETTING AROUND THE AREA

BEYOND THE LAKE DISTRICT

Looking beyond the Lake District there are lots of ways of using public transport in various areas as well as accessing by train or bus. There are a number of special bus services available including -

- **106 Partnership** (*www.106bus.co.uk*) this a bus service between Penrith and Kendal, via Shap and Tebay, and funded by local Parish Councils and other local organisations.
- **563 Bus Service** - this is a bus service, which operates between March and November between Penrith and Kirkby Stephen.
- **Western Dales Bus** (*www.westerndalesbus.co.uk*) has bus services for Sedburgh, Kirkby Stephen and surrounding area linking Kendal. and Penrith.
- **AA 122 Hadrian's Wall Country Bus**.
- In the Peak District -

  The Peak Link 272 Bus Service links Sheffield with Castleton via Hathersage and Edale.

  The train service between Manchester and Sheffield passes through Edale, Hope, Hathersage and Grindleford.
- **Long Mynd and Stiperstones Shuttle Bus** in Shropshire.
- **Sherpa Bus Service** around Yr Wyddfa (Snowdon).
- **Aviemore Adventurer 30** - bus services from Aviemore to Cairngorm car park.

In 2024 the website *www.railwalks.co.uk* was set up to offer a wide network of walking routes from British train stations and is calling on hikers to add their favourites - well worth checking out.

Wherever you are, look out for details of local public transport systems!

Above: Train at Hathersage station.

Right: Aviemore Adventurer 30 bus.

42

ACCOMMODATION

ACCOMMODATION

For those visiting the Lake District there is a huge variety of accommodation available. Looking for accommodation should form part of the planning for a trip, whether as a base for a number of trips or as an overnight stopover while en route to the next stage. The Lake District is made up of a number of valleys radiating out, generally, from its centre and it can be critical to be in the right valley to aid access to the various areas.

Details of accommodation in the valleys such as hotel, bed & breakfast, self-catering accommodation and camping and caravan sites can be found online or in consultation with one of the Tourist Information Centres.

There are a number of hostels around the area with details available as follows -

- **Youth Hostel Association** - the long established organisation with details on *https://www.yha.org.uk*
- **Independent Hostels** - UK's largest network of Bunkhouses, Hostels and Camping Barns - *https://independenthostels.co.uk*

There are a number of **Camping Barns** located around the Lake District - these provide basic self-catering accommodation in traditional buildings. Details of these can be found on the website *https://www.lakelandcampingbarns.co.uk*

The Mountain Bothy Association (MBA) is an organisation which looks after bothies; these provide basic, self-catering accommodation, across the UK and particularly in Scotland. There are three bothies in the Lake District -

- Mosedale Cottage in Swindale in the Far Eastern Fells.
- Lingy Hut on **High Pike** in Northern Lakes.
- Warnscale Bottom above Buttermere.
- There is also Greg's Hut on Cross Fell, in the Pennines.

Full details of the MBA are available on the website *https://www.mountainbothies.org.uk*

WILD CAMPING

Wild camping is technically not permitted anywhere in the Lake District without prior permission from the landowner.

There is, however, a long tradition of wild camping in the Lake District but it is important to know the difference between true wild camping and illegal fly camping.

Parking in campervans and motorhomes is not considered wild camping and you should plan ahead to check where you can park.

Wherever you pitch, please remember that the landowners or their representatives have the legal right to order you to break camp and move on.

ACCOMMODATION

Here are some rules!

Stay out of sight and for only one night

- A wild camp pitch should be above the highest fell wall and should not be noticed by anybody else.
- This means staying away from any buildings or other wild campers.
- Don't camp next to streams or springs to avoid contaminating the water.
- Choose a dry pitch rather than digging drainage ditches around a tent or moving boulders.
- Arrive late in the day (dusk) and move on at dawn.

Keep your group small and be prepared to change your plans

- Many traditional wild camping locations are attracting unsustainable numbers of campers so please remain true to the wild camping ethos of being completely inconspicuous with a tent that blends in.
- If there are two tents already in your spot then you will need to move on – these special places cannot sustain large numbers of campers.

Wild camp, don't fly camp

- If your planned pitch is not above the highest fell wall this is illegal fly camping - not wild camping.
- Camping in car parks or on roadside verges is not allowed at any time.
- No permission is given for camping in valleys, by lakeshores or any lowland area unless it's on an official campsite.

Travel light

- A well-prepared rucksack should contain enough equipment for a basic overnight stay.
- If the rucksack is not big enough and you need more gear, that is an indication that an official campsite will be a better option.
- Use a small and lightweight tent that blends into the landscape - part of the enjoyment really is experiencing unspoilt landscapes.

Don't light fires or BBQs

- Don't light any fires even if there is evidence that fires might have been lit.
- Fires can cause a lot of damage and risk starting uncontrollable wild fires.
- We all need to play our part in protecting this precious environment.
- The right equipment and stocking up on good camp food using a lightweight camping stove is the way to do it.

ACCOMMODATION

Leave no trace

- Leave no litter - this includes not burying any litter and, if possible, removing other people's litter if you find it.
- Perform toilet duties at least 30 metres from water and bury the results with a trowel.
- Carry out everything you carried in.
- Carry out tampons and sanitary towels. Burying them doesn't work as animals dig them up again.
- Leave the campsite as you found it or in a better state!

At all times, help protect the environment and respect other visitors and communities.

The above is the situation as in 2025 and may change. More details are on the following websites - Lake District National Park Authority - *https://www.lakedistrict.gov.uk/visiting/where-to-stay/wild-camping* British Mountaineering Council - *https://thebmc.co.uk*

HAVE A PLAN AND COME BACK SAFELY

Millions of people visit the Lake District each year. Most of these will be visiting the towns and villages in the area and their various attractions. Some will venture on low level walks such as to Friar's Crag on the side of Derwentwater and along the old railway line between Keswick and Threlkeld, whilst others will venture up the fells from **Catbells** to **Scafell Pike** and many in between. Most people walk but there is a large range of other activities: rock climbing, fell running, scrambling, sailing, canoeing, paddleboarding, paragliding, going down mines, amateur radio, bird watching and many more.

Each and every one of these activities gives much pleasure, however that pleasure can be ruined by an incident that could be related to an accident or illness, or to carelessness, inexperience or bad luck - either within or outside of your control. This is when the local emergency services and in particular the mountain rescue teams are around to help - but it is best if you can avoid needing such help in the first place.

When there is an accident it would be great to be able to wind the clock back ten seconds or a minute or a few hours and start again - but you can't do that! You need to try to anticipate moments when things could happen and plan for and avoid them - often these could involve a combination of factors. This is helped by a mixture of knowledge and experience and, linked to that, thinking ahead.

60% of accidents are considered as avoidable and one should give appropriate consideration to the following -

- **Gain the right knowledge about the area and route** -
  - See chapter 4 and familiarise yourself with the area.

- **Give appropriate consideration to the weather** -
  - Think ahead and consider what conditions you will encounter, especially on the tops of the fells. The weather can be hot as well as cold - sunny as well as torrential rain and snowstorms - windy and calm - and much more.

There are a number of useful weather forecast websites available on the internet
https://www.lakedistrictweatherline.co.uk
https://www.metoffice.gov.uk/weather/specialist-forecasts/mountain/lake-district
https://www.yr.no/weatherforecast

Examples of decision making -
see walk **WF3** when two people on **Seatallan** were encountered who had set off at 5.00 am in anticipation of a storm later in the day.
or walk **SF4** with delaying the walk over **Crinkle Crags** etc to the following day - resulting in a stunning day.
and **SF6** with walking the lower fells on day one and the higher fells on the much better day two.

HAVE A PLAN AND COME BACK SAFELY

✓ **Wear the proper clothing and equipment**
- The weather as well as the terrain will dictate what clothing and equipment you will need.
- You should consider clothing for the summits of the fells as well as the more sheltered valleys.
- When the winter comes it can be a completely different ball game on the fells and ice axes and crampons should be considered along with learning how to use them effectively.
- Good and appropriate footwear is so important as a "little slip" and a twisted ankle can lead to all sorts of problems.
- One of the pieces of equipment one is likely to have is a mobile phone and this will be so important in an emergency! Ensure that it is fully charged at the start of the day. You should consider its primary purpose is as a phone and other uses such as taking photographs, information source, digital map, sending out posts on Facebook, Instagram, emails, should be kept to a minimum. Consider putting the phone on flight mode which uses less energy.

✓ **Maintain a First Aid Qualification or Knowledge** -
- If anything goes wrong on the fells any external help, such as a mountain rescue team, is likely to be some distance (and time) away.
- What happens just after an accident can have a profound effect on the outcome and if one is proficient in First Aid this can help enormously for a casualty.
- For someone on their own, extra care should be considered when out on the fells.

✓ **Have you a Plan A and a Plan B and a Plan C?** -
- Having a plan for the day's activity is a good thing and you can bring information together to help plan a safe and enjoyable day out.
- Some may not have a fully-fledged plan but an idea of what they want to do.
- You might have a number of plans depending how the weather is and how the party is coping.
- Plan A was possibly put together with good weather in mind but the day has dawned with torrential rain and you may want to look at a Plan B or just don't go out onto the fells.
- Remember those fells will be there on another day - the important thing is to ensure you are there to go out as well.

Have a look at the website - *www.Adventure Smartuk* - which is full of information to help on this.

Accidents can happen in many ways and those involved with mountain rescue teams have a vast experience of what can go wrong. Have a look at the book published in 2024 by Bob Bennett entitled "A History of Mountain Search and Rescue in the Lake District" to give an idea of rescues and accidents over the years.

There is the perennial issue of gaining experience and knowledge by going out on the fells in all weather. One is always learning and gaining information about an area as well as new techniques and equipment.

The vast majority of people enjoy the Lake District fells with no problems but a little planning and forethought can enhance time on the fells and help to avoid incidents needing mountain rescue teams.

DETAILS AND TALES OF THE FELLS

Early morning view of Buttermere (Walk **WF4**).

This is the core of the book with details about the various fells around the Lake District.

- ▲ This is split into the seven areas used by AW for his guides.
- ▲ The fells are described in the order in which they were ascended over 2023.
- ▲ For each fell or group of fells details are given as follows -
  - ◆ Brief details about the fell or group of fells.
  - ◆ Details of access by public transport or other means.
  - ◆ The story by the ascensionist(s) with the date ascended.

To find out about a particular fell, refer to the index at the back of the book and that will give details on which page(s) the information is contained.

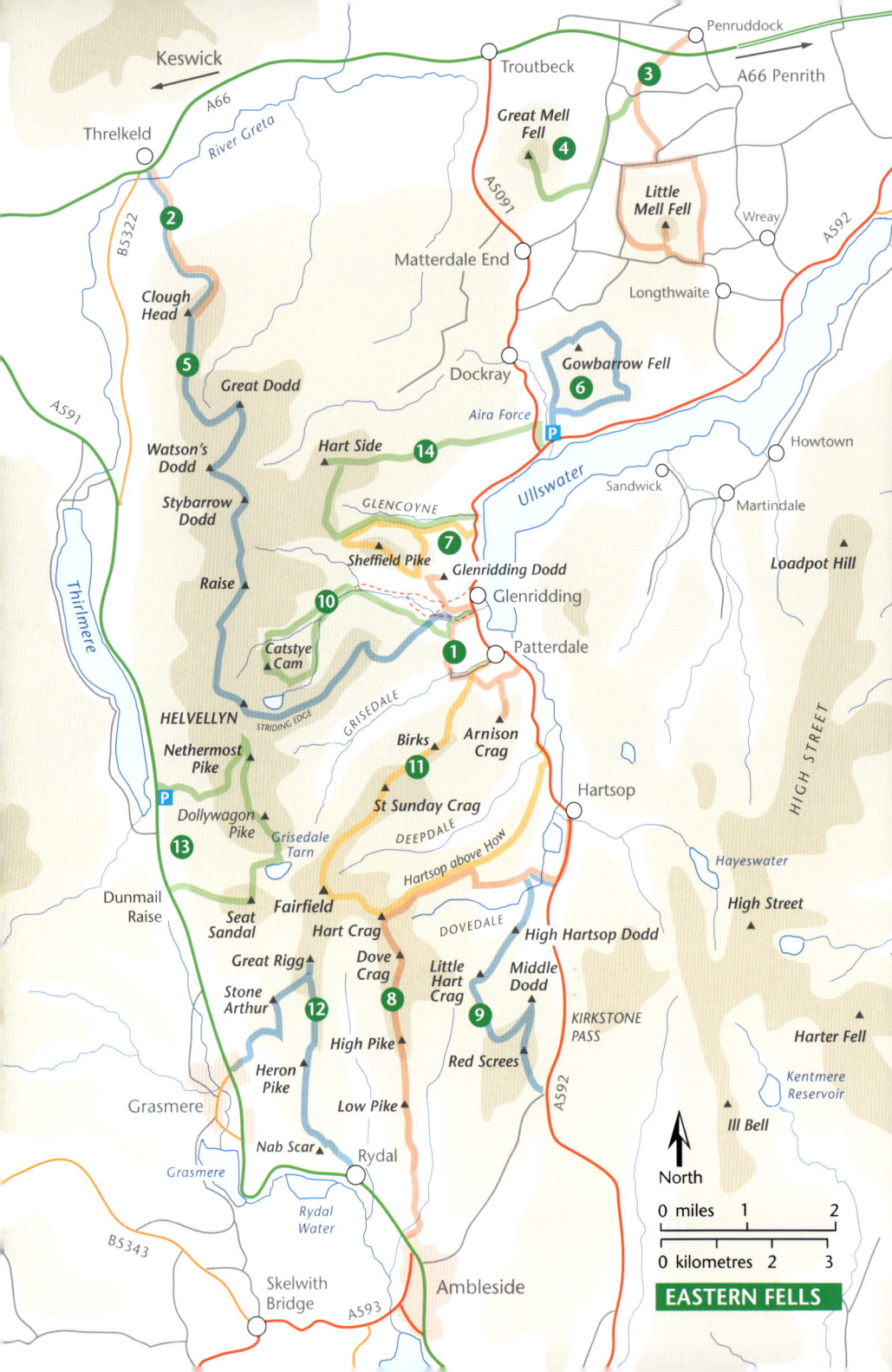

EVMC WAINWRIGHT CHALLENGE - EASTERN FELLS - 2023

1. **ARNISON CRAG and GLENRIDDING DODD**
   Chris Kenyon - 04/02/2023

2. **CLOUGH HEAD**
   Ron Kenyon - 11/03/2023

3. **LITTLE MELL FELL**
   Jane Meeks, Gary Baum and Rona, with visiting collie Skye - 18/03/2023

4. **GREAT MELL FELL**
   Jane Meeks with Rona with visiting collie Skye - 23/03/2023

5. **BIRKHOUSE MOOR, HELVELLYN, WHITE SIDE, RAISE, STYBARROW DODD, WATSON'S DODD, GREAT DODD and CLOUGH HEAD**
   Jon Ginesi - 04/04/2023

6. **GOWBARROW FELL**
   Mary Volume - 19/03/2023

7. **SHEFFIELD PIKE**
   Chris Kenyon - 07/05/2023

8. **HARTSOP ABOVE HOW, HART CRAG, DOVE CRAG, HIGH PIKE and LOW PIKE**
   Ron Kenyon - 18/05/2023

9. **RED SCREES, MIDDLE DODD, LITTLE HART CRAG and HIGH HARTSOP DODD**
   Chris and Ron Kenyon - 29/05/2023

10. **CATSTYCAM**
    Eric Parker - 06/06/2023

11. **BIRKS, ST SUNDAY CRAG, FAIRFIELD, HART CRAG and HARTSOP ABOVE HOW**
    Al Davis and Tara - 20/07/2023

12. **STONE ARTHUR, GREAT RIGG, HERON PIKE and NAB SCAR**
    Chris Kenyon - 26/08/2023

13. **SEAT SANDAL, DOLLYWAGGON PIKE and NETHERMOST PIKE**
    Gary Baum, Jane Meeks and Rona - 30/08/2023

14. **HART SIDE**
    Al Davis and Tara - 08/10/2023

EASTERN FELLS

This area is located between the Ullswater valley to the south and east, the Grasmere and Thirlmere valleys to the west and the A66 (Penrith to Keswick road) to the north.
Helvellyn dominates the area and forms part of the Helvellyn Ridge which stretches along the western side. To its south, **Fairfield** and **Dove Crag** continue the ridge line to the top of Kirkstone Pass. Ridges drop away and can be used to create horseshoe walks around the valleys below. To the east, the outliers of **Great Mell Fell, Little Mell Fell** and **Gowbarrow Fell** give fine viewpoints both into and out of the Lake District.

View of the Eastern Fells from Red Screes on Christmas Day 2006.

EASTERN FELLS

1   ARNISON CRAG and GLENRIDDING DODD

These fells are quite low, compared to the neighbouring summits, with **Arnison Crag** by Patterdale and **Glenridding Dodd** overlooking its namesake Glenridding. **Arnison Crag** can be linked to **Birks** and **St Sunday Crag** and an ascent of **Glenridding Dodd** can be linked with **Sheffield Pike**.

 Glenridding (NY 386 169) and Patterdale (NY 396 159) can be reached on the 508 bus service between Penrith and Windermere, between March and November, otherwise just between Penrith and Patterdale.

 The 509 bus service goes from Keswick to Patterdale then along by Ullswater to Lowther Castle and Penrith on a Saturdays, Sundays and Bank Holidays, between March and November.

Chris Kenyon - 04/02/2023
I caught the 508 bus service from Penrith to Patterdale then went up **Arnison Crag**. *I was really pleased to see a red squirrel on the way up and had a good view from the summit. A pleasant walk then led to the Grisedale Valley and over by Lanty's Tarn to Glenridding. There followed a quick blast up* **Glenridding Dodd**, *with no time to linger on top, as I had to trot down, back to Glenridding, to catch the bus to Penrith.*

View of Ullswater from Arnison Crag (Walk **EF1**) - *photo Chris Kenyon.*

DETAILS AND TALES OF THE FELLS

2   CLOUGH HEAD

This is the large lump of a mountain overlooking Threlkeld and is at the north end of the Helvellyn Ridge. It can be ascended on its own or linked with adjoining summits such as **Great Dodd** or the start of a traverse of the Helvellyn Ridge linking with transport at the far end.

　　　　　The X4/X5 bus services between Penrith and Keswick give access to Threlkeld (NY 324 254) and direct access to Clough Head.

A through trip can be linked using -

　　　　　The 555 bus service from Keswick to Windermere which passes by Thirlmere at Stanah (NY 317 189), Swirls Car Park (NY 315 170) or Wythburn (NY 324 136) and Dunmail Raise (NY 326 117).

　　　　　The 509 bus service from Keswick, by Dockray (NY 393 216) and Glenridding (NY 386 169) to Penrith, via Patterdale, on Saturdays, Sundays and Bank Holidays between March and November.

　　　　　The 508 bus service which goes from Penrith to Windermere (between March and November - otherwise just Penrith to Patterdale) via Glencoyne (NY 386 189) and Glenridding (NY 386 169) on the A592 by Ullswater.

Ron Kenyon - 11/03/2023
Winter conditions were lurking about with a fall of snow on the Lake District fells, though there seemed to be much more elsewhere in the country. After taking the skis out onto Hartside, on the Pennines, with a trip up Fiends Fell, I thought it would be good to ascend one of the Wainwrights on skis. I saw a video made by a friend blasting down off **White Side***, near* **Helvellyn***, on his snowboard, so that was a possibility, but that would need two buses - or there was* **Clough Head** *with a bus just to Threlkeld. There were some odd looks directed at me when carrying the skis through Penrith and catching the 9.15am X5 to Keswick. I got into conversation with a young chap from Nottingham who was well kitted out and heading for the Central Lakes with* **Scafell Pike** *and* **Great Gable** *in his sights. He was an engineer and loved to escape to the fells.* **Blencathra** *appeared with some winter garb and then* **Clough Head***, with what looked like a fine snow line down its left-hand side. Decision time came at the Threlkeld turning - let's go for* **Clough Head** *I decided and off I got.*
The road up to Newsham was followed to eventually gain the fell and the path up with **Clough Head** *looming above. I put the skins on the skis and chatted to the various folk who came past. One was running the Bob Graham Round at the end of May and was having a training run to Dunmail Raise and back. A local lass was having a walk up onto Threlkeld Knotts – Sheffield was mentioned and she said she had gone to university there and was keen on the heptathlon. She had trained at Don Valley Stadium when a young, and a somewhat small and keen, lass called Jessica Ennis appeared and trained there! From the Old Coach Road, I skinned up and leftwards. The runner was now well up near the top of the slope which I was looking to ski down.*

EASTERN FELLS

Clough Head - Skis ready for action (Walk **EF2**).

This was in the area where my son and I were involved in a minor avalanche some years ago – but that is another tale! The terrain was initially good to skin up but eventually was rather bare of snow so it was time to carry the skis to the top. It was quite busy (in **Clough Head** terms) on the fell. I met two young chaps from Yorkshire on the summit - one of whom had fallen off a roof with 53% skull damage and a punctured lung and, in hospital, he had 22 pipes coming in and out of him. After three days he had had enough of hospital and went home! He later went to see the doctor who had first seen him - he knocked on a door and when the doctor opened the door he was looking downwards expecting to see his patient in a wheelchair - but he was standing - the doctor was gobsmacked! Anyway, there he was with 14 Wainwrights to do and off to complete a round over the Dodds and back to Dowthwaite Head (and four Wainwrights). As they set off for **Great Dodd** I told his friend to look after him - although I think he would have looked after himself.

It was time to go down and I found the way into the top of the snow slope. Skis on and across onto the slope and, with trepidation, I made the first turn. This went well and the snow was great, feeling powdery but firm. With some back-sliding and gentle side-slipping to avoid some rocks and boulders it was a great descent of about 1,000 feet which made the whole trip worthwhile.

Back to the track then I descended by Newsham and the road back to Threlkeld and enjoyed a welcome pint at the Salutation Inn before catching the bus back to Penrith.

DETAILS AND TALES OF THE FELLS

3   LITTLE MELL FELL

This is the smaller of the two Mell Fells, which are located between the A66 (Penrith – Keswick road) and the A592 road by Ullswater. Outliers of the main summits, these give fine views in all directions. Composed of glacial waste, these summits are rather pudding shaped. **Little Mell Fell** is approached from the top of the road passing over the col to its south.

An ascent can be linked with the nearby **Great Mell Fell** and it is also possible to create a through route from the A66 to the A592 Ullswater road.

There is a triangle of bus services in the area with –

    The 508 bus service from Penrith by Ullswater - Watermillock (NY 445 227) – to Patterdale and Windermere.

    The X4/X5 bus services between Penrith and Keswick - the closest point is at Penruddock (NY 427 276) from where it is possible to approach through Stoddah and Thackthwaite.

    The 509 bus service from Keswick to Penrith, via Patterdale, on Saturdays, Sundays and Bank Holidays between March and November - which passes **Great Mell Fell**.

    There is also the Ullswater Hopper bus service which is well worth investigating.

Little Mell Fell summit - Jane Meeks with Rona and Skye (Walk **EF3**) - *photo Gary Baum.*

EASTERN FELLS

Jane Meeks, Gary Baum, Rona and visiting dog Skye - 18/03/2023

From the bus stop outside the Herdwick Inn, in Penruddock, we followed the path taking great care crossing the A66 through to Stoddah. Then we took the path through the deer farm to the road at Thackthwaite. Turning right then left, at the first road junction, we followed the road and then the track over the east flank of **Little Mell Fell** *to join the road on the south side - which leads up to the hause. From here the permitted track up* **Little Mell Fell** *is obvious, and is used to ascend to and return from the summit. As you ascend, you soon go through a gate. At this point you will see a path heading off leftwards. This was the path taken after we had returned from the summit. It leads to a series of small roads that hug the fell on its west flank taking one back to Thackthwaite, to complete a circumnavigation of* **Little Mell Fell**. *We then retraced our steps back to Penruddock.*

4   GREAT MELL FELL

This is the larger of the two Mell Fells, which are located between the A66 (Penrith – Keswick road) and the A592 by Ullswater. Outliers of the main summits, these give fine views in all directions. Composed of glacial waste, these summits are rather pudding shaped. **Great Mell Fell** is approached from the north or south sides but is relatively close to the A66 (Penrith to Keswick Road).

An ascent can be linked with the nearby **Little Mell Fell** and it is possible to create a through route from the A66 to the A592 Ullswater road.

There is a triangle of bus services in the area with –

    The 508 bus service by Ullswater.

    The X4/X5 bus services between Penrith and Keswick - bus stop at Troutbeck (NY 388 272) and Penruddock (NY 427 276).

    The 509 bus service from Keswick to Penrith, via Patterdale, on Saturdays, Sundays and Bank Holidays between March and November - which passes **Great Mell Fell**.

    There is also the Ullswater Hopper bus service which is well worth investigating.

DETAILS AND TALES OF THE FELLS

4   GREAT MELL FELL - continued

Jane Meeks, Rona and visiting collie Skye - 23/03/2023
From the bus stop outside the Herdwick Inn in Penruddock, we followed the path to Stoddah, taking great care crossing the A66. A rather hidden footpath gate, just past a concrete road, led to a footpath, through the woodland, then the deer farm, to the Matterdale road, where we turned left. After a mile we reached the vehicle track which goes up towards the fell.
This is the start of the route up **Great Mell Fell** *and there are often several vehicles parked here.*
We followed the track up to the second gate allowing entry onto the fell. On through this we took the path leftwards. After a few minutes we then turned right onto the obvious path heading steeply and directly up the fellside. We then followed this path through the wonderful scattered old woodland to the top with its amazing views.
We retraced our steps to return.

Wind-blown trees on Great Mell Fell (Walk **EF4**).

EASTERN FELLS

5 BIRKHOUSE MOOR, HELVELLYN, WHITE SIDE, RAISE, STYBARROW DODD, WATSON'S DODD, GREAT DODD and CLOUGH HEAD

Birkhouse Moor overlooks the village of Glenridding and is an outlier of **Helvellyn,** being linked by the well-known rocky ridge of Striding Edge. The classic corrie, with Red Tarn, is formed with Striding Edge on the left and Swirral Edge on the right and at the back there are the cliffs below the summit of **Helvellyn**. On the right, along the ridge from Swirral Edge, is the shapely **Catstycam**.

Northwards along the Helvellyn Ridge from **Helvellyn** is a classic walk going over **White Side**, **Raise**, **The Dodds** (**Stybarrow Dodd**, **Watson's Dodd** and **Great Dodd**) then **Clough Head**.

Given the right conditions, there can be good skiing along the ridge including use of the ski tow on **Raise**. The full Helvellyn Ridge provides a fine outing but it can be done in segments and from either side.

Helvellyn Ridge - Shadow on Striding Edge (Walk **EF5**) *photo Jon Ginesi.*

5   BIRKHOUSE MOOR... - continued

On the east side -

The 508 bus service goes from Penrith to Windermere (between March and November - otherwise just to Patterdale) passing through Glenridding (NY 386 169).

The 509 bus service goes from Keswick to Penrith, via Patterdale, on Saturdays, Sundays and Bank Holidays between March and November.

On the west side the 555 bus service goes from Keswick to Windermere, along by Thirlmere, with stops at Stanah (NY 317 189), near Sticks Pass, and Swirls Car Park (NY 315 170).

At the north end of the Helvellyn Ridge are the X4/X5 bus services between Penrith and Keswick passing through Threlkeld (NY 324 254) giving access to **Clough Head** and beyond.

Jon Ginesi - 04/04/2023
*I caught the 508 bus service to Glenridding then went up by Mires Beck and onto **Birkhouse Moor**. I continued onwards to the Hole in the Wall then followed Striding Edge to **Helvellyn**. The junction at Helvellyn Lower Man led down to **Whiteside** and **Raise** then through the '**Dodds**' to **Clough Head**. The final "down" was to the Old Coach Road and I made my way on an indefinite path to Newsham then along the road to catch the bus back from Threlkeld.*
A good, long, classic day.

6   GOWBARROW FELL

Gowbarrow Fell is a very accessible fell, just above Aira Force, next to the A592 by Ullswater. It is encircled by a path as well as a fine, albeit often wet, path along its summit ridge with an exceptional view from the southern subsidiary summit of Green Hill.

Aira Force is where many people go to enjoy the waterfalls and the area around Aira Beck as well as the café. This popularity also draws quite a few up onto Gowbarrow Fell.

The 508 bus service goes from Penrith to Windermere (between March and November - otherwise just to Patterdale) passing by Aira Force (NY 399 199).

The 509 bus service goes from Keswick to Penrith, via Patterdale, on Saturdays, Sundays and Bank Holidays between March and November. This passes through Dockray (NY 393 216) and by Aira Force (NY 399 199).

There is the Ullswater Hopper bus service in the summer months.

The Ullswater Steamers sail up and down Ullswater stopping at the boat landing at Aira Force.

6   GOWBARROW FELL

Mary Volume - 19/03/2023
I took the 508 bus service to Aira Force and joined the crowds going up Aira Beck until, well up the footpath, there is a footpath which branches right and up onto fell. There is now a well-established path (courtesy of Fix the Fells) which leads to the summit. The path continues over and down by the east flank and gives a pleasant gradual way back to Aira Force. After enjoying the very impressive waterfall of Aira Force and views of Ullswater both from the summit of **Gowbarrow Fell** *and from the path descending to my starting point, I then found I had time to spare to take the lakeside path to Glenridding. It was too early in the year for me, but if you time this walk right you can enjoy the brilliant displays of daffodils that inspired Wordsworth's famous poem over 200 years ago.*

7   SHEFFIELD PIKE

Sheffield Pike overlooks the north side of the valley above **Glenridding** and has fine views down the valley and towards **Helvellyn**. **Glenridding Dodd** is an outlying summit to its east and its ascent can easily be combined with an ascent of **Sheffield Pike**.
To its west is the col of Nick Head which gives access to Sticks Pass or Glencoynedale. The area around Nick Head is above the old Greenside Mines.

Ascents can be made from Glenridding (NY 386 169) and Glencoyne (NY 386 189) beside Ullswater. These are accessible, throughout the year, using the 508 bus service between Penrith and Patterdale and from Windermere, between March and November.

Glenridding (NY 386 169) and Glencoyne (NY386 189) can be reached by using the 509 bus service, which runs between March and November, during the summer, between Keswick and Penrith, via Patterdale.

Sheffield Pike with a view over Ullswater (**EF7**) *photo Chris Kenyon.*

7   SHEFFIELD PIKE - continued

Chris Kenyon - 07/05/2023

It was Coronation Bank Holiday Sunday so I hoped **Sheffield Pike** would be quiet. There was also the issue of the Fred Whitton Cycle Challenge passing by as well - but this turned out not to be a problem. I took the 508 bus service to Glencoyne where people were enjoying the lake in the good weather. There were however some paddle boarders who were not wearing life jackets - needless to say this is a dangerous activity, especially when one considers that a paddle boarder, without a life jacket, sadly drowned nearby recently.

I then went up past Seldom Seen, through the woods, then (as advised by AW) turned left and up to the South East Ridge of **Sheffield Pike**. To the left was **Glenridding Dodd** and, rightwards, my path, which I ascended although it was faint in places. There were lovely views with lunch at the subsidiary summit of Heron Pike then some boggy ground to the main summit. I headed on downwards over some more boggy ground to Nick Head then down the fine path through Glencoynedale and back to the road and bus back to Penrith.

Considering it was a bank holiday Sunday I saw relatively few people.

Lunch time on Heron Pike *(Walk* **EF7***) photo Chris Kenyon.*

EASTERN FELLS

8 HARTSOP ABOVE HOW, HART CRAG, DOVE CRAG, HIGH PIKE and LOW PIKE

These fells are linked to the main ridge between Kirkstone Pass and **Fairfield. Dove Crag** and **Hart Crag** are on the main ridge with **Hartsop above How** dropping eastwards between Deepdale and Dovedale and **High Pike** and **Low Pike** on the ridge dropping south from **Dove Crag** to Ambleside.

They can be incorporated in horseshoe walks of valleys, with especially **High Pike** and **Low Pike** being part of the well-known Fairfield Horseshoe.

 The 508 bus service runs from Penrith to Windermere, between March and November, and gives access to the Brotherswater/Deepdale area.

 There are numerous buses in the Ambleside area giving access to various places on the south side of the area.

Ron Kenyon - 18/05/2023
I wanted to make use of the 508 bus service over Kirkstone Pass before the service was temporarily closed on 5th June for road works on Kirkstone Pass.
I would suggest taking the bus to Bridgend, in Deepdale, and ascending **Hartsop above How** *along its length from there. However I wanted to climb a rock climb on Gill Crag, just below the summit of* **Hartsop above How**, *so I took the bus to Brotherswater Inn. From there I went through the Syke Side campsite to Hartsop Hall then up into Dovedale.* **Hartsop above How** *is on the ridge and just past the final gate/wall into the valley I headed up "into the sky" and eventually reached the crag. I climbed the Main Slab Route to the Perch - a most delightful, easy rock climb up the centre of the main slab on amazing holds. Above, the path along the ridge was soon gained and I proceeded onwards along the ridge over* **Hartsop above How** *and up to* **Hart Crag**. *The major ridge path of the Fairfield Horseshoe now led to* **Dove Crag** *and a welcome snack. I just had the descent to Ambleside but I remembered this from the Fairfield Horseshoe Fell Race when the ridge descent seemed to go on forever - taking in* **High Pike** *and* **Low Pike**. *I met three Air Cadets who were out on their fourth day and seemed to have been put through the mill but were enjoying the day with great views over Windermere. Eventually I made my way through Charlotte Mason College to the bus stop nearby and returned by the 555 bus service to Keswick and then Penrith. The 555 bus to Keswick was quite something with table seats and ongoing displayed information about the next stops.*

DETAILS AND TALES OF THE FELLS

9   RED SCREES, MIDDLE DODD, LITTLE HART CRAG and HIGH HARTSOP DODD

These fells are just to the west of Kirkstone Pass and access can be helped by approaching from the top of the pass and climbing **Red Screes**. **Middle Dodd** is on the ridge coming off **Red Screes** and **High Hartsop Dodd** is on the ridge coming off **Little Hart Crag**.
All four summits can be done as a horseshoe from Brotherswater.

 The 508 bus service travels between Penrith and Windermere, by Brotherswater and over Kirkstone Pass, between March and November and may be used to access the area.

Chris and Ron Kenyon - 29/05/2023
Whitsun Bank Holiday Monday - where to go? We decided against the Buttermere area and with the bus over Kirkstone Pass stopping for four weeks from 5th June we decided to head in that direction with **Red Screes** *and beyond in mind. On the 9.32am 508 bus service from Sandgate, in Penrith, for Windermere, numbers gathered but it was not full. Car parking along the way seemed to be filling up, especially in Glenridding.*
We disembarked at Kirkstone Pass summit and collected ourselves for the ascent of **Red Screes**. *There were some rock climbers on Kirkstone Buttress, off to the right. We made our way up the well-made track up* **Red Screes** *to eventually gain its summit and a superb viewpoint.*
After refreshment and contemplation it was down to **Middle Dodd** *then back along a track and down to the head of Scandale then up to the impressive summit of* **Little Hart Crag**.
A pleasant descent then followed to **High Hartsop Dodd** *meeting with a family group en route upwards. There followed a rather steeper descent to gain the valley floor and the Brotherswater Inn for welcome refreshment before the bus back to Penrith.*

Group enjoying fine weather on the top of Little Hart Crag (Walk **EF9**).

EASTERN FELLS

10 CATSTYCAM

Catstycam is at the opposite end of Swirral Edge to its larger neighbour, **Helvellyn**; its rather distinctive triangular shape can be seen from the valley. Overlooking Kepplecove, it dominates the approach path from Greenside Mines to Red Tarn and can be approached by the east ridge. However a much more interesting approach is from the old dam, at Kepplecove Tarn, up the north-west ridge. This is rather indistinct in places but eventually gains the fine summit with views into Red Tarn corrie with **Helvellyn** behind. One can then go along the iconic Swirral Edge to **Helvellyn**. Conversely the summit can be approached from **Helvellyn** via Swirral Edge.

The 508 bus service, between Penrith and Patterdale (to Windermere (March to November) can be taken along the Ullswater valley to Glenridding.

If staying in the Keswick area, the 509 bus service can be taken on a Saturdays, Sundays and Bank Holidays from March to November, to Glenridding, and the Helvellyn Ridge can be crossed into the Thirlmere valley, returning to Keswick on the 555 bus service.

Eric Parker - 06/06/2023
I took the 73 bus service to Glenridding then walked up by the Greenside Mines to the old dam in Kepplecove. The north-west ridge of **Catstycam** *always seems a grind but eventually the summit and "that view" was gained before dropping down the east ridge and back down by Greenside Mines to Glenridding and the bus.*

11 BIRKS, ST SUNDAY CRAG, FAIRFIELD, HART CRAG and HARTSOP ABOVE HOW

The long ridge from Kirkstone Pass over **Fairfield** and **Helvellyn** to **Clough Head** separates the Ullswater valley from the Rydal, Grasmere and Thirlmere valleys. Coming off the section between **Fairfield** and Kirkstone Pass are a number of ridges dropping into the valleys which can provide excellent horseshoe rounds.
The large lump of **St Sunday Crag** overlooks the head of Ullswater, with **Birks** being well worth a deviation from the main track from the valley. A fine ridge, over Cofa Pike, leads to the broad summit of **Fairfield**.
Hart Crag is just to the east of **Fairfield** and these two form part of the popular walk and fell race over the Fairfield Horseshoe, from the south.
Hartsop above How is a long ridge dropping down from **Hart Crag** between Deepdale and Brotherswater, to Bridgend, on the valley road.

The 508 bus provides a service from Penrith to Patterdale throughout the year and beyond to Windermere, passing by Deepdale, between March and November.

11 BIRKS, ST SUNDAY CRAG, FAIRFIELD, HART CRAG and HARTSOP ABOVE HOW - continued

Al Davis and Tara - 20/07/2023

Overcoming my personally hypocritical view of contributing to a sustainability challenge – dubious in view of the miles I have driven this year in pursuit of the Munros – Tara and I took the 508 bus to the Grisedale road end for a splendid day.

The Deepdale Horseshoe was our objective first over **Birks** *to* **St Sunday Crag** *and along the ridge to* **Fairfield***. On the main ridge and part of the Fairfield Horseshoe we went over to* **Hart Crag** *and down by* **Hartsop above How** *then down to Bridgend in time for the 5.20pm bus back to Penrith ... which didn't arrive. So we set off walking to Patterdale in the hope that the 6.20pm bus might exist. A passing car stopped – Mark Houlding and Lee Markle had been climbing at Runestone Quarry and offered a lift. An ethical dilemma ensued – was this allowed within the sustainability rules – but the dog was knackered so we accepted.*

12 STONE ARTHUR, GREAT RIGG, HERON PIKE and NAB SCAR

Nab Scar, **Heron Pike** and **Great Rigg** are on the ridge which forms one half of the popular Fairfield Horseshoe.
Stone Arthur is on the side of the ridge overlooking the Grasmere valley and can be climbed on its own or with the other summits on the ridge.
The ridge walk can also be linked by getting off the bus at the top of Dunmail Raise, ascending **Seat Sandal** and **Fairfield** and descending the ridge to Rydal.

 The 555 and 599 bus services travel along the Rydal/Grasmere valley road giving access to the area.

Chris Kenyon - 26/08/2023

The forecast was dubious so I took the buses, via Keswick, to Grasmere. I went up **Stone Arthur** *(it was a bit difficult to find the actual top) then the weather improved and I went up onto* **Great Rigg** *(brilliant views). I continued down along the ridge over* **Heron Pike** *and* **Nab Scar** *but then saw the rain clouds coming in. The rain started halfway down* **Nab Scar***. Down I went to Rydal where I waited at the bus stop for 30 minutes (in the rain) - no bus! I started walking to Grasmere then the bus went past (I had missed the connection in Keswick anyway). The rain stopped, the next bus came and I got the connection to Keswick and home to Penrith.*
Good day though the transport took rather longer than expected. Excellent views from the ridge!

Bus at Kirkstone Pass.

13 SEAT SANDAL, DOLLYWAGGON PIKE and NETHERMOST PIKE

Seat Sandal is often climbed in combination with its neighbour **Fairfield**.
Dollywaggon Pike and **Nethermost Pike** are at the south end of the Helvellyn Ridge and are usually climbed with their bigger neighbour, **Helvellyn**. The ridges dropping off to the east, into Grisedale, make interesting routes and should be considered in one's plans.

 These summits are near the top of Dunmail Raise which can be accessed by the 555 bus service, between Keswick and Windermere, which runs along the west side of the Helvellyn Ridge and over Dunmail Raise.

 On the east side of the Helvellyn Ridge is the Ullswater valley through which the 508 bus service travels from Penrith to Windermere (just to Patterdale between November and March).

 On Saturdays, Sundays and Bank Holidays, between March and November, the 509 bus service from Keswick to Penrith, via Patterdale, is worth considering if staying in the Keswick area.

 These buses give the options to climb and descend from the same valley or make a crossing of the Helvellyn Ridge, from one valley to another.

13 SEAT SANDAL, DOLLYWAGGON PIKE and NETHERMOST PIKE continued

Gary Baum, Jane Meeks and Rona - 30/08/2023

Seven hours from door to door for two and a half hours on the hill doesn't sound like the most efficient use of time but it was a lovely day out. The now familiar 8.31am X4 bus from Penruddock was followed by the 555 bus from Keswick to Dunmail Raise. The ridge up **Seat Sandal** was ascended, then we went by Grisedale Tarn to **Dollywaggon Pike** and **Nethermost Pike** and along the ridge and then down to Wythburn Church, in Thirlmere.

The return 555 bus from Wythburn Church was a few minutes late so we missed our connection in Keswick. However an hour or so of people watching and drinking coffee in the outdoor Booths café was not a great hardship.

14 HART SIDE

This summit is on the subsidiary ridge, off to the side of **Stybarrow Dodd,** and overlooks Glencoynedale, by Ullswater. It can be accessed from **Stybarrow Dodd** and/or **Sheffield Pike** or just climbed on its own.

It is well worth visiting Birkett Fell. This was named in honour of Lord Norman Birkett who, in the early 1960s, helped to stop the raising of the level of Ullswater, by Manchester Corporation who wanted to use the lake as a reservoir - something which would have changed it forever.

The 508 bus service travels from Penrith to Windermere (just to Patterdale, between November and March) by Glencoyne and Glenridding.

On Saturdays, Sundays and Bank Holidays between March and November, the 509 bus from Keswick to Penrith, via Patterdale, is worth considering if staying in the Keswick area. This gives the possibility of traversing over the Helvellyn Ridge to Thirlmere to then catching the 555 bus service back to Keswick.

Al Davis and Tara - 08/10/2023

We took the 508 bus service from Penrith which dropped us at the lane leading up Glencoynedale. The track gently leads up past the aptly named Seldom Seen cottages eventually topping out at Nick Head. Rather than the obvious higher level route over Greenside, we opted for the delightful track leading round the head of Glencoynedale. This took us past the rear entrance to Greenside Mine, created as an escape route from the mine.

The track, while delightful, is also mainly downhill in this direction and to tick off our hill it was necessary to hack steeply up the featureless hillside to regain the ridge. **Hart Side** stands in splendid isolation well away from the main ridge so was very quiet.

Without the need to head back to a car, we headed north across Watermillock Common towards Aira Force and the bus back home.

EASTERN FELLS

The ski slope on Clough Head with Blencathra behind (**Walk EF2**).

A welcome selection of beers at the Brotherswater Hotel (Walk **EF9**).

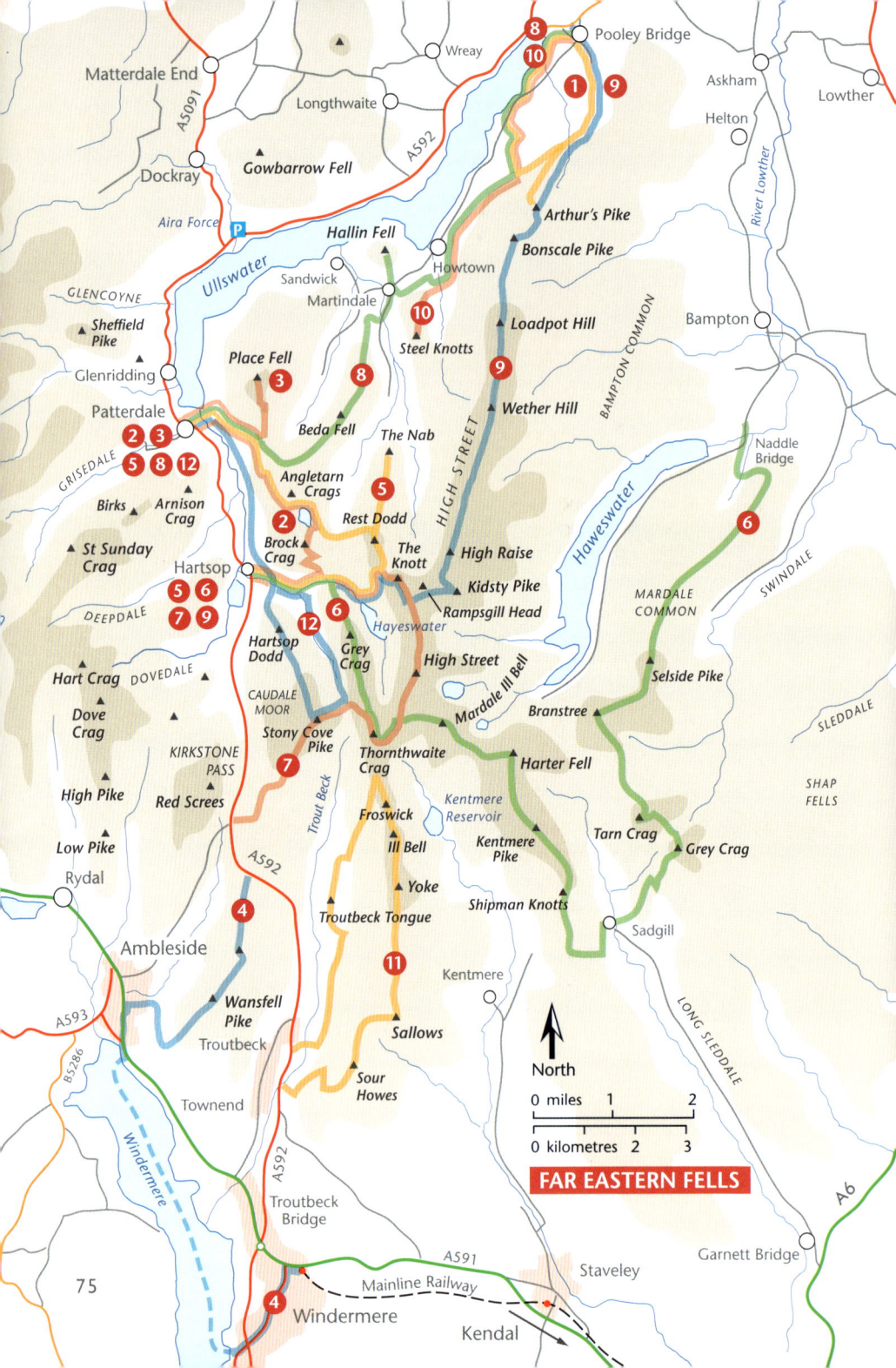

EVMC WAINWRIGHT CHALLENGE - FAR EASTERN FELLS - 2023

1. **ARTHUR'S PIKE**
   Chris and Ron Kenyon - 20/01/2023

2. **BROCK CRAG and ANGLETARN PIKES**
   Chris Kenyon - 20//04/2023

3. **PLACE FELL**
   Mary Volume - 13/05/2023

4. **WANSFELL**
   Chris and Ron Kenyon - 24/05/2023

5. **REST DODD and THE NAB**
   Chris Kenyon - 27/05/2023

6. **SELSIDE PIKE, BRANSTREE, TARN CRAG, GREY CRAG, SHIPMAN KNOTTS, KENTMERE PIKE, HARTER FELL, MARDALE ILL BELL, THORNTHWAITE CRAG and GRAY CRAG**
   Ron Kenyon - 1-2/06/2023

7. **CAUDALE MOOR (Stoney Cove Pike), THORNTHWAITE CRAG, HIGH STREET and THE KNOTT**
   Mary Volume - 03/06/2023

8. **BEDA FELL and HALLIN FELL**
   Mary Volume - 26/07/2023

9. **RAMPSGILL HEAD, KIDSTY PIKE, HIGH RAISE, WETHER HILL, LOADPOT HILL, BONSCALE PIKE and ARTHUR'S PIKE**
   Al Davis and Tara - 26/07/2023

10. **STEEL KNOTTS**
    Chris Kenyon - 09/09/2023

11. **SOUR HOWES, SALLOWS, YOKE, ILL BELL, FROSWICK and TROUTBECK TONGUE**
    Mary Volume - 13/09/2023

12. **HARTSOP DODD and CAUDALE MOOR**
    Kevin Atherton - 17/09/2023

FAR EASTERN FELLS

FAR EASTERN FELLS

These fells lie on the eastern extremities of the Lake District.

To the north and west of the area is the A592 which links Penrith and Windermere, by Ullswater and over Kirkstone Pass.

Well to the east is the A6 between Kendal and Penrith, over Shap Fell, that links with the Howgills to the east of the M6.

The main feature of the area is the line of the Roman Road (High Street) from Galava (at Ambleside) to Brocavum (at Brougham, near Penrith) which traverses over the broad ridge with the highest point on **High Street**.

The popular and accessible summits of **Place Fell, Hallin Fell** and **Angletarn Pikes** lie between the High Street Ridge and Ullswater.

Mardale, just east of the High Street Ridge, contains Haweswater which is the reservoir created by the Manchester Corporation in 1880s.

At the head of Haweswater is the imposing **Harter Fell** from which the valleys of Longsleddale and Kentmere drop away southwards towards Kendal.

High Street and Small Water from Harter Fell (Walk **FEF6**).

FAR EASTERN FELLS

1   ARTHUR'S PIKE

Arthur's Pike overlooks the lower reach of Ullswater and gives a pleasant walk from Pooley Bridge with the added interest of the Cockpit, an impressive and interesting stone circle on Moor Divock, as well as the Roman Road along the High Street Ridge. There is a stunning viewpoint just north-west of the summit.
Its ascent can be linked to nearby **Bonscale Pike**, with a possible descent to Howtown, or along the ridge to **Loadpot Hill** and beyond.

   The 508 bus service, between Penrith and Windermere, goes through Pooley Bridge. Note this bus service is only between Penrith and Patterdale from November to March.

   The Ullswater Hopper bus service goes through Pooley Bridge and Howtown.

   The Ullswater Steamers operate up and down Ullswater calling at Pooley Bridge and Howtown.

Walking along the Panorama Walk on Arthur's Pike with view over Ullswater and the Helvellyn Range beyond (Walk **FEF1**).

74

DETAILS AND TALES OF THE FELLS

1   ARTHUR'S PIKE - continued

Chris Kenyon and Ron Kenyon - 20/01/2023
We had **Arnison Crag** in mind when we went down for the bus in Sandgate, in Penrith. We knew there were some issues with roadworks but the Cumbria County Council website indicated that the buses were going through to Patterdale. When we got onto the bus we found out that this was not the case as there were roadworks just beyond Waterfoot and the bus just went to Pooley Bridge. With a change of plan necessary we put **Arthur's Pike** in our sights.

We disembarked at the Howtown road junction, before Pooley Bridge, and went up a rather slippery and icy road to Roehead. We met some friends at the top who had ventured there with their vehicles for a collective dog walk. We had a good chat and they set off down (with some trepidation) and we set off up the track onto the fell.

It is possible to go by the Cockpit stone circle but we cut the corner en route for **Arthur's Pike**. It was a glorious, though chilly, day and generally firm underfoot - it can be quite boggy across here. We joined the main track, from the stone circle, then went across the beck and upwards. When ascending there is a direct route to the summit but it is best to take a right-hand path which ascends and looks over the lake and beyond and is a well-named Panorama Walk. The summit may be seen up to the left but continue just past the path up to the summit and look for a large cairn signifying "THE" viewpoint. Retrace one's steps and gain that summit.

There are various routes back but it is perhaps best to descend along the Panorama Walk with views in the other direction. The main (The Ullswater Way) track, lower down, heads to Howtown and we joined and followed this with another fine view at Wainwright's Sitting Block. This is next to a stream, which is a good place for a bite to eat. It is possible to follow the track to Howtown from this point, however we took the track past Seat Farm and Cross Dormont then down to the road. Just past Waterfoot we followed the path by the campsite and along by the lake and back to Pooley Bridge.

There was time for suitable refreshments and then we joined the bus which was parked there waiting for us.

2   BROCK CRAG and ANGLETARN PIKES

These two summits encircle the classic Angle Tarn above the hamlet of Hartsop.

   The 508 bus service between Penrith and Windermere gives access to various locations along the valley. Remember the bus does not go over Kirkstone Pass between November and March.

Chris Kenyon - 20/04/2023
I took the 508 bus service from Penrith to Hartsop then headed up **Brock Crag** - great views. I continued along to Angle Tarn and up onto **Angletarn Pikes** where I sat in the sun for lunch. I went onward and down to Boredale Hause then on to Patterdale but I just missed the bus. I decided to walk to Glenridding and catch the steamer to Pooley Bridge. I hadn't been on the steamer for years and it was a very scenic cruise down the lake. From Pooley Bridge I boarded the bus back to Penrith. A grand day out.

FAR EASTERN FELLS

3   PLACE FELL

Place Fell is the imposing fell on the east side of Ullswater, opposite Glenridding, with approaches by Side Farm at Patterdale. There are a number of ways of climbing it - the normal route is by Boredale Hause then up to the summit. For the more adventurous, there is a way up the front face topping out near the subsidiary summit called The Knight. It is also possible to walk along by the lake to near Sandwick to then follow Scalehow Beck, continuing on up to the summit. Probably the best way is to take the steamer to Howtown and walk along by the lake, or over **Hallin Fell**, to Sandwick, up Scalehow Beck and down by Boredale Hause.

  The 508 bus service gives access to Glenridding and Patterdale.

  The Ullswater Steamers sail up and down Ullswater stopping at Glenridding and Howtown as well as at Pooley Bridge.

Mary Volume - 13/05/2023
I caught the 508 bus to Patterdale then walked up and down **Place Fell** *via Boredale Hause.*

The Ullswater Steamer with Glencoyne and Sheffield Pike behind, from Place Fell.

DETAILS AND TALES OF THE FELLS

4   WANSFELL

Wansfell is positioned right above Ambleside and can be gained from various directions as follows:

> up the front overlooking the town.
> from the village of Troutbeck, close to Limefitt Park.
> from the road over Kirkstone Pass.

 One can make use of the 508 bus service, between Windermere and Penrith, over Kirkstone Pass, between March and November.

View from Wansfell towards the Central Lakes (Walk **FEF4**).

Chris Kenyon and Ron Kenyon -   24/05/2023
Only one summit but quite an expedition! We caught the 508 bus service and asked the young bus driver if he could drop us at a gate, just beyond the top of Kirkstone Pass, near the path along the ridge of Wansfell. Just before we set off, the bus driver stood up and gave the following useful announcement   -

| ✖ | No Seat Belts | ✖ | No First Class | ✖ | No Refreshments | ✖ | No Toilets |
| ! | | | If you want a heated seat – sit on a seat at the rear of the bus, which is above the engine! | | | | |

We met a couple from Gloucester looking to climb **Red Screes**, **Middle Dodd**, **Little Hart Crag** and **Hartsop Dodd** and they left the bus (with Go-Pro ready for action) at the top of Kirkstone Pass. Descending to Windermere, we were looking for the gate and found a good stopping point with the summit of Wansfell, 150m above us, in the not-too-far distance.

It was rather boggy across the first section then gradually we gained the main summit and all the time the views around developed. We could see Wansfell Pike, at the other end of the ridge, with rather more people on it and we made our way along to it. This is 5m lower than the main summit but the view is spectacular and is a much more popular top to attain from Ambleside or Troutbeck. After a bite to eat and look at "that view" we continued westwards and dropped down with the view over Windermere and eventually through Blue Hill Wood, gaining the A591 near Hayes Garden, on the edge of Ambleside.

A short walk took us to the steamer landing at Waterhead and after a quick drink and some cake we were on the steamer heading for Bowness-on-Windermere passing Wray Castle, Low Wood, Brockhole, The Steamboat Museum and into a busy Bowness. Our next objective was the railway station which is quite a hike upwards (we could have taken the bus) and we set off. Eventually we found the station, hidden next to Booths and Lakeland. We had pondered on a quick blast up Orrest Head (AW's first Lakeland summit) but time did not allow so we awaited the train. A lot of people gathered with us to eventually board and take the train to Oxenholme - this was certainly a first for Chris and me. There was a bit of a wait at the station but eventually we were being whisked up the main train line to Penrith.

5   REST DODD and THE NAB

These two fells overlook the head of Bannerdale - one of the two valleys in Martindale. **Rest Dodd** is just off the ridge leading from **Angletarn Pikes** to **The Knott**. **The Nab** is along the ridge to the north of **Rest Dodd**. The land below **The Nab** is privately owned and there is no permitted access from Bannerdale onto **The Nab** and so its summit should be approached from **Rest Dodd**.

 The 508 bus service from Penrith to Patterdale travels by Hartsop, between March and November, and can be used to access the area - or, it can be accessed from Patterdale via Boredale Hawse and **Angletarn Pikes**.

Chris Kenyon - 27/05/2023
It was a lovely sunny day and I caught the 508 bus service to Hartsop. I then walked up to Hayeswater and on up to **Rest Dodd**. *AW was rather dismissive of* **Rest Dodd** *describing it as "a fell of little interest" however it has good views and the bogs were all dry. Then onto* **The Nab** *and a path which dodges peat hags. Back towards* **Rest Dodd** *I took a short cut rightwards to the main track, then went past Angle Tarn and down by Boredale Hause to Patterdale.*

DETAILS AND TALES OF THE FELLS

6   SELSIDE PIKE, BRANSTREE, TARN CRAG, GREY CRAG, SHIPMAN KNOTTS, KENTMERE PIKE, HARTER FELL, MARDALE ILL BELL, THORNTHWAITE CRAG and GRAY CRAG

This is an odd mix of summits covering quite a wide area but it happened due to the location of **Tarn Crag** and **Grey Crag**, next to Longsleddale, which are a long way from any bus or train routes. Similarly **Selside Pike** and **Branstree** are well away from any public transport services as they are located overlooking the southern end of Haweswater.

 The key to accessing this area is the Fellrunner Bus service which acts as a lifeline for the locals around the Eden Valley - in this particular case with the service which runs on a Thursday from Penrith to Burnbanks, below the dam at the northern end of Haweswater. This gives access, by Naddle Valley, to **Selside Pike** and **Branstree** then **Tarn Crag** and **Grey Crag** beyond.

 The fells to the south of the Longsleddale valley - **Shipman Knotts**, **Kentmere Pike**, **Harter Fell** and **Mardale Ill Bell** can be approached from Kentmere. Kentmere can be approached over Garburn Pass from Troutbeck, at the south end of Kirkstone Pass, where the 508 bus service passes by in the summer. This can be linked to a traverse of the Kentmere Horseshoe finishing with **Thornthwaite Crag**, **Froswick**, **Ill Bell** and **Yoke**.

 The 508 bus can be used to approach **Thornthwaite Crag** either from the top of Kirkstone Pass over **Caudale Moor** or up by Threshwaite Cove from Hartsop.

 Gray Crag overlooks Hartsop and can be incorporated into a walk to or from Hartsop linking with the 508 bus.

Ron Kenyon - 01 – 02/06/2023
I realised early on that accessing **Tarn Crag** *and* **Grey Crag** *above Longsleddale could create problems. I had thought there was a bus along the A6 over Shap Fell but it goes via Tebay. Then a little leaflet about the fantastic Fellrunner Bus service appeared and this showed that there was a bus service to Burnbanks, on a Thursday. This would get me a bit closer but would it be close enough? Well let's give it a try with the idea of an overnight camp in the Longsleddale area.*
I set off on the bus at Sandgate, in Penrith, with the one other passenger and driver and we made our way by Lowther, Shap, Rosgill and Bampton Grange to Burnbanks - collecting various ladies (and a gent) who were heading for a few hours in Penrith. It was also possible to catch up on some of the local craic.
From Burnbanks I headed up by Naddle Farm and the centre of the RSPB activities there. Continuing up onto the left (east) ridge of the valley eventually took me to Hare Shaw (a Birkett) and **Selside Pike**. *Across the valley I could see a very distant looking* **Mardale Ill Bell** *which I was planning to pass over the next day. I eventually reached the summit where there were two people in residence.*

FAR EASTERN FELLS

Selside Pike from Hare Shaw (Walk **FEF6**). Jay, a chance meeting on the fells.

One was one of two brothers who were the first to complete all the Birketts (and receive pints from Bill Birkett at the ODG) - he had also recently completed the Munros and was helping his pal with the Wainwrights.
Branstree came and went then I headed down into Mosedale with **Tarn Crag** and **Grey Crag** in sight - but concern was rising about camping with the area being so dry. **Tarn Crag** led on to **Grey Crag** and I met a couple from Cockermouth, with their daughter and future son-in-law. They had been to visit the location, near Windermere, which is to be used for the reception for the wedding in 2024 and they thought, being in the area, that it was a good chance to climb these two summits. The ground looked very dry and I was still concerned about camping or the possible need to escape to the valley. However a small stream, across the path, solved everything and I decided to set up camp. What a location with a view south towards Kendal and beyond.
I could hear the resident snipe and I hoped I was not disturbing the bird. I awoke to see the sunrise at about 3.00am and I was amazed to see the full moon setting, thus creating a moonset, in the other direction.
In the morning the ridge on the other side of the valley did not look too bad as I set off downwards. I met someone, from Whitehaven, who had driven the two hours to Sadgill to walk the Longsleddale Horseshoe. I dropped into the valley then climbed up the other side where I met Jay whom I had seen on Selside yesterday. He had discovered fell walking in 2015 and was now ticking off odd summits for his second round of the Wainwrights - with other summits in his sights that day. He was also working on other challenges in the UK with Nuttalls and County Tops (highest one in Kent is in a lady's back garden) and pondering on the Munros - all the best Jay!
Shipman Knotts was a bit of a shock to the system when planning this route. I had initially forgotten about it then realised it was a Wainwright and had to change plans. Anyway, here I was plodding up it. Here also was a young lady from Kendal who was having a quick blast round the Kentmere Horseshoe - she started at 7.30am and it was not quite 11.00am!

6   SELSIDE PIKE, BRANSTREE etc - continued

I felt I had cracked the ridge and made my way onwards. On the summit of **Kentmere Pike**, I met a young man from Lancaster, who did not have a car and had taken the train to Windermere and was also working his way through the Wainwrights without a car.

When approaching **Harter Fell** I met a group of young ladies who were discussing their favourite ice creams (liquorice was mentioned) in anticipation of a visit to Kimi's Gelato at Staveley.

Scampering up from Nan Bield Pass were three fell runners, who were involved with the Steve Parr Round. After **Mardale Ill Bell** the pacer of another fell runner was waiting for his pal, also on the Steve Parr Round, and was doing the out-and-back to Harter Fell. I later saw them on **Thornthwaite Crag**, where his pal was desperate for more water on such a hot day. He was 10 hours into what would be a 30 hour plus schedule! I only had one to go with **Gray Crag** along the ridge, to the north from **Thornthwaite Crag**, then it was down (and down) to Hartsop.

It was a while until the next bus so I went along to the Brotherswater Inn for some liquid refreshment - it felt so much hotter in the valley without a breeze. At the bus stop, a lady from the Isle of Wight was waiting. She did not have a car and was staying at the Patterdale Youth Hostel and working her way through the Wainwrights. She, like me, had concerns about how to get to **Tarn Crag** and **Grey Crag** - but that was for the future - for me it was the past.

Fellrunners on Mardale Ill Bell on the Steve Parr Round (Walk **FEF6**).

7   CAUDALE MOOR (Stoney Cove Pike), THORNTHWAITE CRAG, HIGH STREET and THE KNOTT

Caudale Moor is to the east of the summit of Kirkstone Pass with **Thornthwaite Crag** (and its fine summit cairn) on the other side of Threshthwaite Mouth. Nearby is the fell that gives the ridge its name - **High Street**. Can you visualise the Roman soldiers going over here nearly 2,000 years ago? **The Knott** is an outlier overlooking Hayeswater, in the valley below, by which the path leads down to Hartsop.

  The 508 bus service travels between Penrith and Windermere, over Kirkstone Pass and by Hartsop, between March and November.

Mary Volume - 03/06/2023
*I took the 508 bus service to the top of Kirkstone Pass (it always feels cheating gaining this height before setting off) then walked over **Caudale Moor** to **Thornthwaite Crag** and onto **High Street**. I continued on downwards, with a short ascent of **The Knott**, then down by Hayeswater to Hartsop and the bus back home.*

FAR EASTERN FELLS

Caudale Moor from Raven Crag (Walk **FEF7**).

8   BEDA FELL and HALLIN FELL

Hallin Fell is a lovely fell, overlooking Ullswater and Howtown, with a distinctive cairn on its summit. **Beda Fell** is a long ridge between Boredale and Bannerdale, in the Martindale area, leading along to **Angletarn Pikes**.

    The 508 bus travels from Penrith into the Ullswater valley to Pooley Bridge and Patterdale.

    During the summer there is the Ullswater Hopper bus service which travels to Howtown.

    The Ullswater Steamers sail up and down Ullswater stopping at Glenridding, Pooley Bridge and Howtown giving options to link Howtown to Pooley Bridge or to go back to the head of the lake at Glenridding.

Mary Volume - 26/07/2023
*I took the 508 bus to Patterdale, then walked over by Boredale Head to **Beda Fell** and along to Martindale Hause. After a blast up **Hallin Fell** I walked back to Pooley Bridge and met Al Davis and Tara on the 508 bus back to Penrith, after their day on the High Street Ridge (Walk **FE9**).*

82

DETAILS AND TALES OF THE FELLS

9   RAMPSGILL HEAD, KIDSTY PIKE, HIGH RAISE, WETHER HILL, LOADPOT HILL, BONSCALE PIKE and ARTHUR'S PIKE

These fells are along the northern end of the High Street Ridge. This broad ridge, between Martindale and the Lowther Valley, would have been traversed by the Romans many years ago.

View north from Loadpot Hill with Blencathra and Skiddaw in the distance (Walk **FEF9**).

     For the **Rampsgill Head** and **High Raise** area (as well as nearby **High Street**) use the 508 bus service between Penrith and Windermere, between March and November, to Hartsop and then walk up the valley by Hayeswater to the High Street Ridge.

     Alternatively one can disembark at Patterdale and ascend over Boredale Hause and continue via Angle Tarn or walk along, by Crookabeck, to Hartsop then up the valley via Hayeswater.

     Arthur's Pike and **Bonscale Pike**, overlooking Ullswater, can be accessed from Pooley Bridge or Howtown with the 508 bus service passing through Pooley Bridge.

     Howtown is accessible using the Ullswater Steamers or the Ullswater Hopper bus service, or by walking from Pooley Bridge.

Al Davis & Tara - 26/07/2023
We took the 508 bus service to Hartsop and ascended by Hayeswater, passing by **The Knott**, *up* **Rampsgill Head** *and the rather dramatic looking summit of* **Kidsty Pike** *to* **High Raise**. *The ridge northwards takes in* **Wether Hill, Loadpot Hill, Bonscale Pike** *and* **Arthur's Pike** *with fine views into the Lakes and the Eden Valley. We returned on the 508 bus back from Pooley Bridge meeting up with Mary Volume on the same bus after her walk (Walk* **FE8**).

83

10   STEEL KNOTTS

Steel Knotts is on the ridge dividing Fusedale from Martindale with **Hallin Fell** at the north end of the ridge with both overlooking the hamlet of Howtown on the side of Ullswater. The south end of the ridge links to **Loadpot Hill** and **Wether Hill** on the High Street Ridge.

    The Ullswater Steamer, which operates up and down the lake, gives access to Howtown

    There is also the section of the Ullswater Way linking Howtown to Pooley Bridge.

    During the summer there is the Ullswater Hopper Bus which travels to Howtown.

Refreshments are available at the Howtown Hotel or on the steamer.

Chris Kenyon - 09/09/2023
I took the 508 bus service from Penrith to Pooley Bridge, but unfortunately it was a bit late and I missed the connection with the steamer. I walked along, initially by the lake, to Howtown then up the ridge to the summit of **Steel Fell**. *Descending back down to Howtown I took the steamer back to Pooley Bridge. Needless to say Pooley Bridge was very busy with lots of people swimming / paddle boarding / kayaking etc.*

11   SOUR HOWES, SALLOWS, YOKE, ILL BELL, FROSWICK and TROUTBECK TONGUE

These fells are at the south end of the High Street Ridge overlooking the valley of Troutbeck and the south end of Kirkstone Pass.

High Street from Selside Pike (Walk **FEF6**).

11 SOUR HOWES, SALLOWS, YOKE, ILL BELL, FROSWICK and TROUTBECK TONGUE - continued

This area is best accessed by the 508 bus service between Penrith and Windermere, over Kirkstone Pass, between March and November.

Mary Volume - 13/09/2023

I took the 508 bus service over Kirkstone Pass and disembarked at the Limefitt Park for an ascent of **Sour Howes** and **Sallows** before continuing up the fine ridge to **Yoke**, **Ill Bell** and **Froswick**. Just before **Thornthwaite Crag** a path drops back down into Troutdale - this is close to the line of the old Roman Road which went from Galava fort (Ambleside) to Brocavum fort (Brougham near Penrith). **Troutbeck Tongue** was then ascended before catching the 508 bus back over Kirkstone Pass.

12 HARTSOP DODD and CAUDALE MOOR

These are the two summits just to the east of Kirkstone Pass.
Caudale Moor is the higher and is closer to the top of Kirkstone Pass. It gives useful access to the High Street Ridge with its relatively easy ascent from the top of Kirkstone Pass.
Hartsop Dodd is the spur dropping off **Caudale Moor** down to the hamlet of Hartsop.

The 508 bus service goes over Kirkstone Pass between Penrith and Windermere, from March to November.

Kevin Atherton - 17/09/2023

I took the 508 bus service from Penrith to Hartsop and made the steep ascent up to **Hartsop Dodd** followed by a duller trudge to **Caudale Moor**. A path was followed eastwards down to a col from where a path led down left into Threshthwaite Cove. A great view was had of Raven Crag up to the left; this is the location of some difficult rock climbs. The path then passes near the large boulder called 'Rolling Rock'. This is a popular bouldering rock climbing venue and on cue, a group of square bouldering mats could be seen in the distance toiling up from Hartsop. From Hartsop, quiet paths lead through attractive woods below Lingy Crag. A footbridge spans the Angletarn Beck, dropping steeply from Angle Tarn, with good views across to the Deepdale area. I carried on through Crookabeck to Patterdale and the 508 bus service back to Penrith.

FAR EASTERN FELLS

Above: Hartsop Dodd (Walk **FEF12**) - *photo Kevin Atherton.*
Below: The 555 bus service going by Waterhead, Ambleside - *photo Stagecoach.*

EVMC WAINWRIGHT CHALLENGE - CENTRAL FELLS - 2023

1. **HIGH RIGG**
   Chris Kenyon - 27/03/2023

2. **HIGH SEAT**
   Chris Kenyon - 02/04/2023

3. **GRANGE FELL and GREAT CRAG**
   Eric Parker - 16/05/2023

4. **WALLA CRAG and BLEABERRY FELL**
   Chris Kenyon - 21/05/2023

5. **RAVEN CRAG**
   Chris Kenyon - 05/06/2023

6. **LOUGHRIGG FELL and SILVER HOW**
   Chris Kenyon - 11/06/2023

7. **SERGEANT'S CRAG and EAGLE CRAG**
   Eric Parker - 12/06/2023

8. **ULLSCARF, ARMBOTH FELL and HIGH TOVE**
   Ron Kenyon - 22/06/2023

9. **TARN CRAG**
   Chris Kenyon - 08/07/2023

10. **STEEL FELL, CALF CRAG, GIBSON KNOTT and HELM CRAG**
    Kevin Atherton - 04/08/2023

11. **LOFT CRAG, PIKE O'STICKLE, HARRISON STICKLE, PAVEY ARK, THUNACAR KNOTT, SERGEANT MAN and HIGH RAISE**
    Jane Meeks, Gary Baum and Rona - 08/09/2023

12. **BLEA RIGG**
    Mary Volume - 29/09/2023

CENTRAL FELLS

The Central Fells occupy the area with Borrowdale to the west, Langdale to the south and the Grasmere and Thirlmere valleys to the east. **High Raise** is very central to the Lake District with the iconic Langdale Pikes to the south.
The ridges eastward lead over **Blea Rigg, Silver How** and **Loughrigg Fell** as well as **Tarn Crag**, **Gibson Knott** and **Helm Crag**.
Northwards is the central ridge linking **Ullscarf** with **High Seat** and **Walla Crag**.

View from Grange Fell with Derwentwater and Skiddaw in the distance (Walk **CF3**).

CENTRAL FELLS

1   HIGH RIGG

High Rigg lies between the Naddle Valley and St John's-in-the-Vale on the ridge stretching from the A66 to where the river goes under the A591, near Thirlmere. Rather overshadowed by its neighbours, it does, however, give a fine walk.

    The closest approach is from the south near Bridge End Farm (NY 315 194) where the 555 Keswick to Windermere bus service passes.

    Alternatively it can be accessed from the X4/X5 Penrith – Keswick bus service on the A66 disembarking at the junction onto the old road, which leads to Burns Farm (NY 315 248).

Chris Kenyon - 27/03/2023
I took the Keswick bus service to Threlkeld (NY 322 254) then walked across the fields to a minor road, near Shundraw, and on upwards past Tewit Tarn (lovely views) to the St John's Church and the Field Centre there. A steep ascent then led up to the summit of **High Rigg**. *Back down to the Field Centre, I then turned left and down by Dale Bottom. From here I followed a path which led up to the Castlerigg Stone Circle and then down the road into Keswick for the bus back to Penrith.*

Summit of High Rigg with Robinson, Grasmoor and Grisedale Pike in the distance (Walk **CF1**)
photo Chris Kenyon.

2 HIGH SEAT

High Seat is well named; perched on the ridge between Derwentwater and Thirlmere, it gives fine views in all directions. It is usually approached from the Derwentwater side but can be reached from the east, up the Shoulthwaite valley, near Thirlmere.

 The 78 bus service operates up and down Borrowdale and can be used to access locations along the valley such as at the junction up to Ashness / Watendlath (NY 268 203).

 The 555 bus service, from Keswick to Windermere, can be used to access Shoulthwaite valley (NY 300 205).

Chris Kenyon - 02/04/2023
The monthly EVMC rock climbing day meet was planned for Shepherd's Crag, in Borrowdale. The idea of taking the bus was mooted and six members of the EVMC took the bus from Penrith, via Keswick, to Lodore (NY 263 188) and Shepherd's Crag nearby.
I made my way along below the crag then ascended the path on its right side to the top of the fell above, beside Upper Shepherd's Crag, to enjoy the view down Borrowdale. I continued onwards, by Watendlath Beck, to the road above then down to Ashness Bridge and that VIEW. It was a stunningly fine day and I decided to make the ascent of **High Seat**, following Ashness Gill to its summit, with fantastic views. I descended back by Ashness Bridge to the road and the bus. I was amazed to see Ron on the same bus after having climbed at Shepherd's Crag and joined him on his way back to Penrith.

EVMC group on the bus at Keswick bound for Shepherd's Crag and beyond (Walk **CF2**).

CENTRAL FELLS

3   GRANGE FELL and GREAT CRAG

These two fells overlook Rosthwaite and the area just beyond the Jaws of Borrowdale. Nice to climb both individually or together, they offer a number of combinations of walks. The two fells are bisected by the track from Rosthwaite to Watendlath.

For **Grange Fell** there is a path going up from the head of Troutdale, to its north. This can be gained:

   from the track leading into Troutdale, by Leathes Hotel.

   by a path near the bridge at Grange.

   from the car park for the Bowderstone.

There are two summits of **Grange Fell** - King's How, to the west, at 392m, and Brund How, to the east, and marginally higher at 415m. The summit of King's How was purchased in memory of the late King Edward VII by his sister Princess Marie Louise and given to the nation - hence its name. There are descents down the west side or by the track between Rosthwaite and Watendlath. For **Great Crag**, access is possible from the track between Rosthwaite and Watendlath, or from Watendlath with paths leading to the summit then on past Dock Tarn and down into Langstrath, with views up this "long valley" into the Central Fells.

There are various bus routes along the valley which can be used but remember the 78 bus goes up and down the main road of the valley and the 77a goes clockwise and through Buttermere. Useful bus stops are as follows: entrance to Troutdale (NY 256 177), Grange Bridge (NY 255 174) and Rosthwaite NY (258 149).

Eric Parker - 16/05/2023
From Keswick I took the 78 bus service to the track leading into Troutdale and followed the path up King's How then over to Brund How, the highest point of **Grange Fell**. *The usual somewhat soggy path took me down to the track between Rosthwaite and Watendlath. I carried on over* **Great Crag** *then down by Dock Tarn to Rosthwaite and the bus back to Keswick.*

Sign at Stonethwaite - starting point for many walks and runs in that area.

92

DETAILS AND TALES OF THE FELLS

4   WALLA CRAG and BLEABERRY FELL

These two fells overlook the north end of Derwentwater and Keswick.
Walla Crag can be accessed from Keswick:

    by the path, from Springs Road, to Rakefoot and up to the summit.
    from the Great Wood car park, below the front face, and either
        o   up left to Rakefoot.
        o   following the path to the right and up Cat Gill.

Bleaberry Fell can be accessed from **Walla Crag** or linked with other summits along the ridge.

    The 78 bus service goes from Keswick to Borrowdale passing near the Great Wood car park (NY 271 214).

    Great Wood car park can be accessed on foot from Keswick either along the main Borrowdale road or via Friar's Crag and Calf Close Bay.

Chris Kenyon - 21/05/2023
I took the bus to Keswick then walked down to the lake and had a coffee at the Theatre by the Lake. Sitting outside in the sun it felt like being on holiday! Then I made my way over to the Borrowdale road and up **Walla Crag** *by Great Wood and Rakefoot. It was very busy on top with folk enjoying lovely views. I continued onward and upward to* **Bleaberry Fell** - *this used to be really boggy but now there is a well-made footpath. I saw very few people beyond* **Walla Crag**. *I continued down back to Rakefoot, then down the path to Springs Farm and by* Castle Head *and back into Keswick.*

View from Bleaberry Fell towards Keswick and Skiddaw (Walk **CF4**).

CENTRAL FELLS

5   RAVEN CRAG

On the east side of **Raven Crag** is a very dramatic crag containing some very difficult rock climbs. With this steep face overlooking Thirlmere, the summit commands a fine view over the lake and **Helvellyn** beyond.

For the full frontal approach, start at Bridge End next to the A591 near Thirlmere. Follow the road over the dam at the end of Thirlmere with **Raven Crag** towering above and ascend the path on the right.

The 555 bus service goes along the side of Thirlmere, between Keswick and Windermere, by Shoulthwaite (NY 300 205) and Bridge End (NY 315 194), at the north end of Thirlmere.

Chris Kenyon - 05/06/2023
*I took the bus to Keswick then followed various paths to Shoulthwaite (would have been better to have taken the bus from Keswick to Shoulthwaite or Bridge End!). I then went up through the woods to the col between The Benn and **Raven Crag**, then followed the track to its top with the great view over Thirlmere. I continued back down the steep "normal" path to near Thirlmere, then across the dam and along the road to the A591 and the bus back to Keswick and Penrith*

View from Raven Crag over Thirlmere (Walk **CF5**).

6   LOUGHRIGG FELL and SILVER HOW

These two popular fells are between Great Langdale and Rydal valleys, overlooking the south side of Rydal Water and Grasmere, and can be approached from either side as well as from Ambleside.

   To the north there are the 555 & 599 bus services passing through Rydal (NY 364 061) and Grasmere (NY 337 076).

   To the south is the 516 bus service from Windermere to Great Langdale, via Skelwith Bridge (NY 344 035) and Chapel Stile (NY 322 055).

Chris Kenyon - 11/06/2023
*I took the bus to Keswick then the 555 bus service to White Moss Common (NY 349 065) next to Rydal Water - busy! I went upwards by Loughrigg Terrace to **Loughrigg Fell** - excellent views. I continued down to the road at the top of Red Bank and along the ridge to **Silver How** - HOT - then down by Allen Bank to Grasmere and the bus back home - everywhere was hot and dry.*

7   SERGEANT'S CRAG and EAGLE CRAG

These two fells dominate the east side of Langstrath with **Eagle Crag**, to the north, presenting its distinctive profile when seen from Stonethwaite. They are actually on a ridge dropping down from **High Raise** and can be incorporated into an ascent of that summit from Borrowdale. **Eagle Crag** is usually approached from Stonethwaite, up the frontal ridge, however in mid-summer this area is covered in deep bracken which can hinder progress.

   The 77, 77a and 78 bus services in Borrowdale take one to the Stonethwaite junction (NY 257 142) and can be used for an out-and-back or else out-and-over to Grasmere or Langdale - taking buses back from over there.

Eric Parker - 12/06/2023
*I took the bus to Stonethwaite, via Keswick, and followed the path, going through the campsite then up the Langstrath valley, on its east side, to Blea (or Gash) Rock, near the popular Blackmoss Pot. I made the steep ascent of the fellside to the top of **Sergeant's Crag**, passing the rock climbing venue of Sergeant Crag Slabs en route. I then went along the ridge over **Eagle Crag**, with the dramatic crag on its north side, then continued onward down the ridge to the valley and along to catch the bus at the Stonethwaite junction.*

Eagle Crag from Stonethwaite.

8   ULLSCARF, ARMBOTH FELL and HIGH TOVE

These fells have a reputation for being damp underfoot but in the middle of June 2023 this was not an issue. They are situated on the main ridge between Borrowdale and Thirlmere and can be approached from either side with the options of traversing from one valley to the other or returning to the same valley.

 There are bus services (77, 77A & 78) running up and down the Borrowdale valley and can be taken to various locations including Stonethwaite junction (NY 257 142).

 The 555 bus service runs by Thirlmere assisting with access to Ullscarf from the south end of the lake at Steel End (NY 322 128), at the entrance to the Wythburn valley.

Ron Kenyon - 22/06/2023
On that bus again, next to a lady looking for sandals in Keswick then a chunky walk. She lives near Penrith and is a keen diver, having moved back from working as a diving instructor in Egypt and was looking for a place to settle back into the UK. On the Borrowdale bus I met a lady badminton player who used to play for the Keswick Badminton Club and we recalled badminton matches of the past. I disembarked at Stonethwaite and made my way up to Greenup Edge. Just below the imposing crag on the side of **Eagle Crag** *I was caught up by a family group heading, they thought, to Blackmoss Pot.*

8   ULLSCARF, ARMBOTH FELL and HIGH TOVE - continued

Their instructions were in the car, however they were having a good time despite me telling them they were in the wrong valley - needless to say they did not have a map! Quite a few folk were enjoying the view from the spectacular Lining Crag while I continued up for a break and refreshment near Greenup Edge. **Ullscarf** *was eventually gained (quite a few false summits) but what a viewpoint! I continued over the* Birketts *of High Saddle and Low Saddle - Low Saddle in particular is a great little summit with a fine view over Watendlath. I went down to Blea Tarn and a water temperature test led to a lovely dip in the tarn - it was quite shallow, and just above the hips, but great to have a refreshing swim. I continued onwards across the relatively dry bog to* **Armboth Fell** *(what a great summit!) then plodded up to* **High Tove** *before dropping down to Watendlath. Unfortunately the café had just closed so it was onwards down the valley and by Lodore to a welcome rehydration with orange juice, lemonade and ice then a pint of beer, crisps and chips at the Borrowdale Hotel before catching the bus back home. Only about 9 miles but with the heat I felt somewhat tired!*

View from Lining Crag with Skiddaw in the distance and Scotland beyond (Walk **CF8**).

CENTRAL FELLS

Summit of Armboth Fell with Blencathra beyond (Walk **CF8**).

9   TARN CRAG

The well-named **Tarn Crag** looks over Easedale Tarn, above Grasmere, with the dramatic Deer Bield Crag to its north, on the side of Far Easedale. It is an outlier of **High Raise** and can be linked with an ascent of **High Raise** and others or climbed just on its own.

    There are various bus services (555 and 599 buses) passing through Grasmere (NY 337 076) from Keswick and Ambleside/Windermere.

Chris Kenyon - 08/07/2023
After the Keswick bus I took the somewhat busy 555 bus to Grasmere. Onward up Easedale, I went over the footbridge and along the path towards Far Easedale. I managed to find the path up the ridge to **Tarn Crag**, *but battled through chest high bracken (remember it is July!) towards the summit. The top is not really obvious but I met a man with a GPS, who found the right general area and I found the cairn. Excellent views. I continued down to Easedale Tarn (more bracken bashing) then back down by Far Easedale.*
The sky went dark, up blew the wind, then there was thunder, lightning and torrential rain - bouncing off the road and bouncing off me! Not far to go to Grasmere - I sat in the bus shelter and dripped dry on the bus back to Penrith

10   STEEL FELL, CALF CRAG, GIBSON KNOTT and HELM CRAG

These fells encircle the valley of Green Burn - the scene for the poem "Michael" by William Wordsworth - to the north of Grasmere.

There is the regular 555 bus service between Kendal and Keswick as well as the 599 bus service between Windermere and Grasmere. These fells can be ascended starting in Grasmere (NY 337 076), The Traveller's Rest (NY 335 089) or at the top of Dunmail Raise (NY 326 117).

Kevin Atherton - 04/08/2023
I took the X4 bus service to Keswick then the 555 bus to the top of Dunmail Raise. The road reaches a height of just under 800 feet at the pass which is the only low level road link between the north and south Lakes. Raise is an old name for a cairn and a large cairn between the carriageways is said to mark the burial place of a Cumbrian king called Dunmail. The steep path up **Steel Fell***, by the fence, joins the north ridge of the fell which is followed to the summit. This route is often taken during the Bob Graham Round.   I then walked west and then south-west around the head of the Green Burn valley and over boggy ground to* **Calf Crag***. This can be tricky to find in the mist but is a good viewpoint across to the very rough fellside leading up to* **Sergeant Man** *and* **Tarn Crag***. A narrowing ridge leads to* **Gibson Knott** *then the fine ridge was followed to the rocky and popular summit of* **Helm Crag***. The highest point is a group of rocks known as the 'Howitzer' or the 'Lion Couchant'. I felt that the project required that the highest point be reached so I carefully scrambled up and down (a feat not accomplished by Wainwright!), then headed down to Grasmere.*
The same buses were taken back to Penrith with time for a drink in the Twa Dogs Inn at the edge of Keswick between buses. A nice sunny afternoon's walk.

11   LOFT CRAG, PIKE O'STICKLE, HARRISON STICKLE, PAVEY ARK, THUNACAR KNOTT, SERGEANT MAN and HIGH RAISE

This is very much the central area in the Lake District with valleys flowing to the east into Great Langdale and Grasmere as well as north to Langstrath and Borrowdale. These tops make up the iconic summits of the Langdale Pikes and surrounding fells.

Access is normally from Great Langdale (516 bus service) from the New Dungeon Ghyll (NY 295 065) however these fells can be accessed from Grasmere (555/599 bus services - NY 337 076) by Easedale Tarn.

There are also possible traverses of this area, for instance from Stonethwaite (NY 257 142) in Borrowdale (77, 77A & 78 bus services) over to Grasmere, then returning by bus (555 bus service) to Keswick, or continuing into Great Langdale and beyond.

CENTRAL FELLS

Jane Meeks and Rona on the summit of High Raise (**CF11**) - *photo Gary Baum.*

Jane Meeks, Gary Baum and Rona - 08/09/2023
This was a day of rather extreme bus travelling giving another lovely day in the fells. We took the early X5 bus to Keswick, getting on in Penruddock, having walked from home for thirty minutes across wet, boggy fields. The bus was very full of excited school children, comparing their new timetables. Then we boarded the 555 bus to Ambleside followed by the 516 bus to New Dungeon Ghyll in Great Langdale. Due to a delay, we only just made our connection in Ambleside, for which we thought we had left ample time. The 516 bus was leaving the bus station as we arrived and we had to run to stop it. Top tip – don't bang on the side of the bus if you don't want to upset the driver!

We started up the Stickle Ghyll (also known as Mill Gill) path but very soon turned onto the leftwards path heading by Dungeon Ghyll, which we followed to **Loft Crag** *and* **Pike o'Stickle**. *We then chose to double back to* **Harrison Stickle** *followed by* **Pavey Ark**, **Thunacar Knott** *and* **Sergeant Man** *before finishing on* **High Raise**. *We descended by Wythburn to Steel End, at the south end of Thirlmere to catch the 555 bus to Keswick and home. The beck on the way down to Steel End provided a welcome dip on what was a very hot day.*

12 BLEA RIGG

Blea Rigg is positioned between Great Langdale and Grasmere and can be accessed from either side being a broad ridge with the Langdale Pikes to the west and **Loughrigg** to the east.

  There are the 555 & 599 bus services which serve the Grasmere area (NY 337 076).

  Great Langdale can be accessed by the 516 bus service between Windermere and the Old Dungeon Ghyll with access in particular to the New Dungeon Ghyll (NY 295 065).

Mary Volume - 29/09/2023
I took the bus to Keswick then the 555 bus service to Grasmere. It was quite mixed weather so I decided not to take in any other fells as I'd already been caught in a heavy shower. I ascended Easedale by Easedale Tarn to **Blea Rigg** and returned the same way via Grasmere and Keswick.

View over Watendlath to the Central Lakes with Great End and Great Gable in the distance (Walk **CF8**).

CENTRAL FELLS

78 bus service travelling through the Jaws of Borrowdale -
photo Richard Burgess.

EVMC group ready for the bus to Shepherd's Crag and beyond (Walk **CF2**).

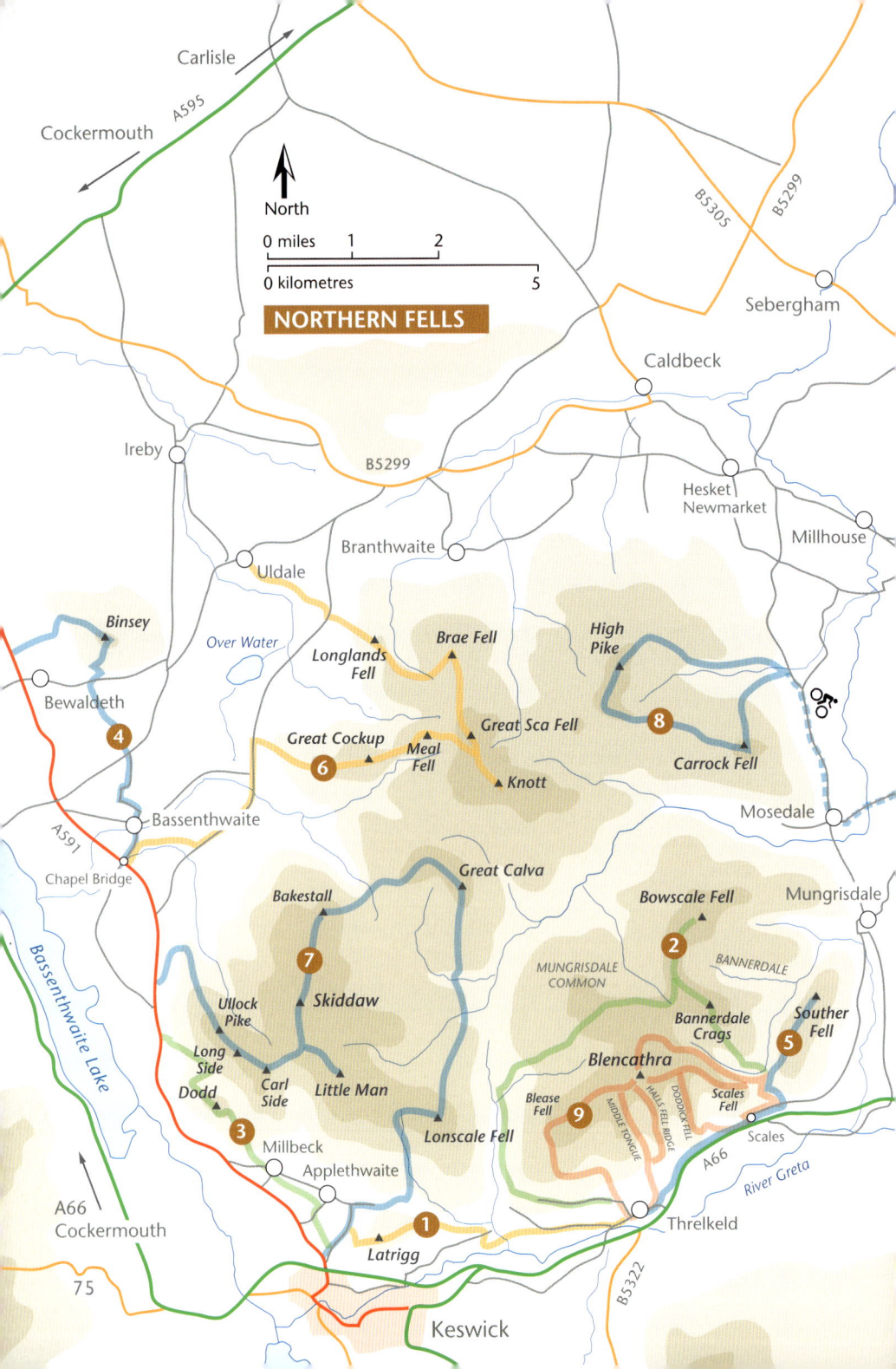

EVMC WAINWRIGHT CHALLENGE - NORTHERN FELLS - 2023

1. **LATRIGG**
   Chris and Ron Kenyon - 17/01/2023

2. **BANNERDALE CRAGS, BOWSCALE FELL and MUNGRISDALE COMMON**
   Ron Kenyon - 14//02/2023

3. **DODD**
   Chris Kenyon - 27/02/2023

4. **BINSEY**
   Chris and Ron Kenyon - 08/04/2023

5. **SOUTHER FELL**
   Chris Kenyon - 27/04/2023

6. **GREAT COCKUP, MEAL FELL, KNOTT, GREAT SCA FELL, BRAE FELL and LONGLANDS FELL**
   Ron Kenyon - 27/05/2023

7. **ULLOCK PIKE, LONG SIDE, CARL SIDE, SKIDDAW LITTLE MAN, SKIDDAW, BAKESTALL, GREAT CALVA and LONSCALE FELL**
   Gary Baum, Jane Meeks, Rona and Barney - 18/08/2023

8. **CARROCK FELL and HIGH PIKE**
   Jane Meeks - 28/08/2023

9. **BLENCATHRA**
   Phil Blanshard, Dave Hellier, John Howarth, Ron Kenyon, Andy Lloyd, Belinda Lloyd, Eric Parker, Ian Phillips, Soo Redshaw and Mary Volume - 16/12/2023

DETAILS AND TALES OF THE FELLS

NORTHERN FELLS

This is the area of fells at the northern edge of the Lake District which includes the 3,000 footer of **Skiddaw** as well as **Blencathra**, on the south side, the central summit of **Knott** with ridges dropping away from it and **High Pike** with **Carrock Fell** on the east side. The area hidden behind **Skiddaw** and **Blencathra** is known as Bac'o'Skidda or Back of Skiddaw.

1   LATRIGG

Latrigg is the very popular summit looking out over Keswick, at the foot of **Skiddaw**. It is best approached, from Keswick, through Fitz Park, and along Spooney Green Lane which crosses the A66 and ascends round the side of **Latrigg** to a car park. This route can also be used to ascend **Skiddaw** by Jenkin Hill. There are various routes from the track to the summit of **Latrigg**. The fell can be traversed before dropping down and either continuing along to Threlkeld by Wescoe or following the old railway line along through the gorge and back into Keswick.

   Access is from Keswick or by using the X4/X5 bus services through Threlkeld.

Chris and Ron Kenyon - 17/01/2023
To get the ball rolling with the EVMC Wainwright Challenge, we took the X4 bus service from Sandgate, in Penrith, and saw various friends using the bus to get through to Keswick. From Keswick bus station we went along Southey Street into Fitz Park and had a look at the new pump track there. We carried on by Brundholme Road and up Spooney Green Lane. There was a map indicating ways up **Latrigg** *with various rounds shown and instead of taking the track round to the left side of* **Latrigg** *we followed a track up and round to the right. There had been some tree removal work here and a gate led us to a path and upwards to gain the summit ridge.*
We decided to carry on to Threlkeld so we went along the ridge and down the east side, into the Greta Gorge. We followed the road through Wescoe with fine views, to the south, with the backdrop of **Lonscale Fell** *and* **Blencathra**. *We reached Threlkeld and, after refreshments at the Threlkeld Coffee Shop, we caught the bus back to Penrith and met up again with the friends we had seen on the bus that morning.*

View from Latrigg with Chris Kenyon on the summit (Walk **NF1**).

NORTHERN FELLS

2   BANNERDALE CRAGS, BOWSCALE FELL and MUNGRISDALE COMMON

A circumnavigation of **Blencathra**.

Bowscale Fell and **Bannerdale Crags** are usually approached from Mungrisdale but, when using the bus, Scales (The White Horse), on the side of **Blencathra**, is probably the best starting point. It is possible to walk or bike from the A66 along to Mungrisdale and start the ascents from there.

Mungrisdale Common is the nondescript fell to the north of **Blencathra** - about which many say – "Why did AW include this one?".

   The X4/ X5 Penrith to Keswick bus services can be used to access Scales (The White Horse) (NY 342 268) or the Mungrisdale (NY 368 273) junction.

In 2024 there was no official bus stop at Scales and the buses did not always stop there for disembarking or embarking. I hope something can be resolved on this. See www.jaggedlakes.co.uk for any updates.

Ron Kenyon - 14/02/2023
I caught the 9.15am X4 bus for Keswick and disembarked at Scales (The White Horse) and made my way up Mousthwaite Comb. I chatted with a local couple on the way up the track. They were out for a quick blast up **Blencathra** *before their children were back home from school.*
I dropped down to the bridge over the River Glenderamackin then went into low gear and headed up **Bannerdale Crags**. *I gradually gained height and the views opened up towards Scales Tarn and* **Blencathra** *as well into the Eden Valley and Eastern Lakes. After a bite to eat at the summit cairn, it was onward to* **Bowscale Fell** *- but then realised I had left my camera, so had to return to the summit to retrieve it - annoying!*
Onward again I eventually reached the shelter on **Bowscale Fell** *and took more refreshment before the final summit -* **Mungrisdale Common**. *Rather surprisingly I saw six people ascending it today. It even has a summit cairn now. AW has a lot to answer for - but it's not as boring as AW said!*
A pleasant descent led down to the path from the Skiddaw House and back along to the road, near the Blencathra Centre. I called into the Mountain Heritage Trust office at the Blencathra Centre and had a chat with the curator there.
During liquid replenishment at the Horse and Farrier in Threlkeld I chatted with a lady and her two daughters (aged 10 & 6) who had just climbed **Blencathra** *and were enjoying well-deserved and welcome ice creams.*
I took the 3.31pm bus back to Penrith ready for the "school's out" clog up in Penrith.

3   DODD

Dodd is attached to the side of **Carl Side** and overlooks Bassenthwaite Lake. It is surrounded by Dodd Wood and there are various forest walks with a café near the road. On the west side of the road is Mirehouse with pleasant gardens and a walk down to the lakeside. AW described the summit as the weirdest summit as it was covered in trees in the 1950s. Those trees have now gone and the view has been transformed.

 The X4, 554 and 553 bus services go along the east side of Bassenthwaite Lake and can be used to reach Dodd Wood (NY 235 280).

Chris Kenyon - 27/02/2023
I caught the X4 bus service, via Keswick, to Dodd Wood and walked up forestry tracks to the summit of **Dodd.** *There are now great views for such a small fell - there were a couple of people on top who were amazed you could see Scotland!*
I went down the other side, via a steep path, between the trees and the forestry road, to the minor road leading to the village of Millbeck. There then followed pleasant walking along a quiet road and field paths to eventually join the Spooney Green Lane path from Keswick up **Latrigg**. *I turned right, over the A66 and went through Fitz Park to the Keswick bus station, with time for a coffee before catching the bus back to Penrith. It was great to be able to make a linear walk and to walk by Millbeck and Applethwaite and to join "that path" on* **Latrigg**.

View over the Lake District from Hall's Fell on Blencathra (Walk **NF9**).

NORTHERN FELLS

4 BINSEY

Binsey is very much an outlier, beyond the Skiddaw group, at the very northern edge of the Lake District. Consequently it has fine views into the Lakes and across the Solway Firth into Scotland.

 The 554 bus service between Keswick and Carlisle, via Wigton, goes along the A591 beside Binsey.

 The X4 bus service passes by Bassenthwaite village on the way to Workington.

Chris and Ron Kenyon - 08/04/2023
Where do you go on Easter Saturday? - Binsey! We took the bus to Keswick and then the 554 bus service which goes from Keswick to Carlisle. Needless to say there were hordes of folk piling onto the Seatoller and Ambleside buses, but only eight onto the 554 bus. We went along by Bassenthwaite Lake, disembarked at the Bewaldeth junction (NY 208 348) and walked along by the A591 to a lane going up onto **Binsey**. *After a pleasant and quiet walk up the fell we met the crowds (but nothing like Catbells!) on the summit. There was a couple from Whitehaven, with parents from Devon, enjoying the summit, and who seemed to be rapidly ticking off the Wainwrights. Another chap was in radio contact with the world and his pals as part of the amateur radio scene - we understand he made 17 contacts with other amateur radio enthusiasts that day.*
After a bite to eat, it was down by Fell End and High Bewaldeth farms to the road from Castle Inn to Ireby. The last time Ron went this way was when doing the Wainwright Relay with Harry Blenkinsop in 1993 - it was the first leg and a hot day and they had just done the Whinlatter Fells and the Skiddaw Fells were to follow. We took the road along to Robin Hood - an interesting name for around here. On the way down to Bassenthwaite a lady and son were letting loose their two horses in a field - one horse was just over a year old and the other was 31 years old!
The Sun Inn at Bassenthwaite beckoned before catching the X4 bus back via Keswick to Penrith. Not a long walk but it was varied and, considering it was Easter Saturday, it was quiet.

Amateur radio operator on the summit of Binsey with Bac'o'Skidda in the distance (Walk **NF4**).

5   SOUTHER FELL

Souther Fell is an offshoot of **Blencathra** overlooking the hamlet of Mungrisdale. It is renowned for the sight of the phantom army, supposedly belonging to Bonnie Prince Charlie, which has been seen along the summit of the fell. It is very steep at its northern end and usually approached from the south, from Scales, via Mousthwaite Comb, though it can be ascended by a circuitous route from Mungrisdale.

   The X4/ X5 bus service between Penrith and Keswick runs by Scales, just west of Threlkeld.

In 2024 there was not an official bus stop at Scales and sometimes the bus driver would not stop here - I hope this can be resolved - check www.jaggedlakes.co.uk for any updates.

Chris Kenyon - 27/04/2023
It was a bit chilly so I decided on a shorter walk today. I took the X4 bus service to Scales, where the driver kindly let me off at the White Horse Inn. Then I headed onward and up by Mousthwaite Comb and along to **Souther Fell**. *There is a cairn, to the side of the ridge, with no particular purpose except perhaps to indicate a good viewpoint - so I sat there, out of the wind, for lunch. I continued onward to the top and then back along above Mousthwaite Comb and down by its west side to the A66. There followed a short walk by the A66 (bit tedious) and then the C2C Cycle Route shortcut to Threlkeld for coffee and cake at the Threlkeld Coffee Shop.*

Fell runners on Knott - with Scotland beyond (Walk **NF6**).

6   GREAT COCKUP, MEAL FELL, KNOTT, GREAT SCA FELL, BRAE FELL and LONGLANDS FELL

Bac'o'Skidda or Back of Skiddaw is the vast area in the Northern Fells with rolling fells and fine views to the north, over the Solway Firth, to Scotland. Central to this area are **Knott** and **Great Sca Fell** with **Meal Fell** and **Great Cockup** dropping away to the west and **Brae Fell** and **Longlands Fell** to the north.

NORTHERN FELLS

From an access point of view there are various bus routes around these fells as follows:

 On the west side by Bassenthwaite - X4 bus service to Workington and 554 bus service, via Wigton, to Carlisle.

 On Saturdays, Sundays and Bank Holidays the 553 bus service travels between Carlisle and Keswick passing through Caldbeck, Uldale and Bassenthwaite.

 The Penrith – Keswick buses (X4/ X5 bus services) go along the south side of the area. These can be used for access from Threlkeld by the Glenderaterra valley, between **Blencathra** and **Skiddaw**.

Ron Kenyon - 27/05/2023
The key to getting into the north side of Northern Fells was with the Caldbeck Rambler 73 bus service which ran on a Saturday (Note this was changed in 2024 to the 554). The first bus from Carlisle was at 7.50am but the first train from Penrith to Carlisle was 7.15am and would not link. Therefore I needed to change direction and get on the 8.10am bus to Keswick and then Bassenthwaite and look to catching the bus at Uldale, to Carlisle, which was at 4.33pm.
So back on the X4 bus service I had chats with two Johns, from Penrith, and also two IT guys from London with **Scafell Pike** and the 6.50pm bus back from Seatoller in their sights.
I disembarked at Bassenthwaite Chapel bus stop (NY 227 316), with another couple from Penrith, and we made our way along roads and a path eastwards. I said cheerio to the couple, who went up the Dash Force footpath for Skiddaw House and Keswick, whilst I carried on to Horsemoor Hills and onto **Great Cockup**.
Upward and onward - I had orienteered around here and it is such a great area with just a map, compass and whistle. I carried onward passing Trusmadoor (magical name and place) and over **Meal Fell**. There were quite a few folk about including a couple of fell runners who whizzed past looking to complete all the Northern Fells, over two days, with a camp somewhere that evening.
A bit of a trudge up **Great Sca Fell** followed and, with loads of time in hand, I decided to add in **Knott** (too close not to do so). What a great central summit in this area, with a fine view covering the Isle of Man, Isle of Whithorn, Galloway Hills to The Cheviot and the Pennines! Back on **Great Sca Fell** I saw the fell runners again. They had just dispatched **Longlands**, **Brae Fell** and **Great Sca Fell** - next, for them, was **High Pike** and **Carrock Fell** and some refreshment in the Mill Inn at Mungrisdale.
There were a couple in the small shelter on Little Sca Fell - they were from Manchester though it turned out that the lass's mum lived in Bassenthwaite and she used to live there so this was her home turf.
A short detour picked up **Brae Fell** before finishing with **Longlands Fell**.
With Uldale (NY 249 369) in sight, I followed a delightful path from near Longlands Farm through fields to arrive at Mae's Café, in the Old School, for suitable refreshment.

DETAILS AND TALES OF THE FELLS

6   GREAT COCKUP, MEAL FELL, KNOTT, GREAT SCA FELL, BRAE FELL and LONGLANDS FELL - continued

The couple I had met on Little Sca Fell *arrived later and we continued our conversation.*
4.33pm was approaching and I had to drag myself away from Mae's to catch the bus. It was a little late, due I would expect to the traffic situation in Keswick (it was Whit Saturday), but eventually I was on the bus making my way through Ireby, Caldbeck, Hesket Newmarket, Sebergham, Welton and Dalston to Carlisle - where a bus was waiting to whisk me on to Penrith.
Good full day and great to get these Wainwrights done!

Great Cockup, Meal Fell and the Northern Fells from Mae's Café (Walk **NF6**).

View from Skiddaw towards Great Calva, Carrock Fell, Blencathra and Lonscale Fell.

NORTHERN FELLS

7   ULLOCK PIKE, LONG SIDE, CARL SIDE, SKIDDAW LITTLE MAN, SKIDDAW, BAKESTALL, GREAT CALVA and LONSCALE FELL

Skiddaw is one of the 3,000 footers in the Lake District and attracts a goodly number of ascensionists. It towers over Keswick and draws people from various directions to its lofty summit. It commands fine views, in particular from its smaller neighbour **Skiddaw Little Man,** over Borrowdale and the Lake District. With its conical shape, **Skiddaw** is very distinctive when viewed from the north and Scotland.
The fine ridge to the west contains **Ullock Pike**, **Long Side** and **Carl Side** with views over Bassenthwaite Lake.
Bakestall is to the north of the main summit overlooking the dramatic Dash Falls area.
Lonscale Fell is to the east of the Jenkin Hill approach to **Skiddaw** but also has interesting approaches from the Glenderaterra Beck valley.
Great Calva is really an outlier of **Knott** in the Bac'o'Skidda area with its distinctive shape, reminiscent of Fujiyama, when viewed from the A66 (Penrith - Keswick road) up the Glenderaterra Beck valley.

These summits can be approached:

Directly from Keswick.

With use of the X4 or 554 bus services along the east side of Bassenthwaite Lake.

The X4/X5 bus services passing through Threlkeld.

Gary Baum, Jane Meeks and Rona - 18/08/2023
After a 25 minute walk to Penruddock we took the usual bus - the X5 - from outside the Herdwick Inn to Keswick, then the X4 bus along Bassenthwaite Lake, getting off just after the Ravenstone Hotel (NY 235298). The steep path up to Ling How starts just to the south of the hotel. The Edge is our favourite way up **Skiddaw** *and takes you over* **Ullock Pike**, **Long Side** *and* **Carl Side**.
We took the right hand of the two paths on the side of **Skiddaw** *and diverted to pick up* **Skiddaw Little Man** *before heading back to the main summit of* **Skiddaw**. *On* **Skiddaw Little Man** *we met two young ladies who were walking the Cumbria Way and who had decided to take a diversion over* **Skiddaw.** *They were heavily laden with camping gear and we almost envied them with their heavy sacks as the wind on the summit tried to blow us off our feet. We continued roughly north over* **Bakestall**, *dropping steeply down to Whitewater Dash, before negotiating the boggy ground leading to that curse of the* Bob Graham Round - **Great Calva**. *We then took the obvious path SSW down to the vehicle track which led us to Skiddaw House. We briefly ventured inside this lovely hostel and were pleased to find the two ladies, we had met earlier, who were staying there for the night.*
We ascended **Lonscale Fell** *by the oddly named Burnt Horse ridge and followed the path by Whit Beck down to Keswick. It felt like a long day - 18 miles and 1,700m of ascent.*

DETAILS AND TALES OF THE FELLS

8   CARROCK FELL and HIGH PIKE

These two summits are at the northern edge of the Lake District with fine views - in particular northwards to Scotland and along the Eden Valley to the east.

   The public transport here is rather limited and use of a bike should be considered.

   The Caldbeck Rambler 73 bus service, between Carlisle and Keswick, used to pass through Hesket Newmarket, but this service was replaced in 2024, by the 553 which goes from Dalston to Caldbeck (NY 324 398), missing out Hesket Newmarket.

   Some 4 miles (6km) from Carrock Fell the X4/X5 bus services follow the A66 between Penrith and Keswick passing the Mungrisdale Junction (NY 368 273).

Jane Meeks - 28/08/2023
Coming from Penrith on the bus (assuming you can get your bike on the bus) or on your bike, there are several options to reach the start of the walk. My cycle from home went past the bus stop outside the old Sportsman's Inn. From there I took the road north through Berrier, past the lovely nature reserve at Eycott Hill. I went straight on at a crossroads and about half a mile further on I took a left turn down the narrow gated road to Mosedale. Turning right I followed the fell road, by **Carrock Fell***, and took the first left turn that led to the ford and footbridge across Carrock Beck (NY 350 350).*
I left my bike here and took the obvious path that leads up onto **Carrock Fell** *from where the route round to* **High Pike** *can be boggy in wet weather. There are a few options to descend* **High Pike** *but it is nice to follow the grassy track that heads over West Fell.*
Once back to the bike I then retraced my way back to the A66.

9   BLENCATHRA

Also known as Saddleback, this is one of the most accessible and popular major summits in the Lake District. It is just north of the A66, towering above Threlkeld. **Blencathra** has, according to AW, a selection of 13 routes up it following ridges and valleys, passing over various summits and converging on the main summit at the top of Hall's Fell Ridge. Stunning views can be had in all directions - a must for all fell walkers in the Lake District.

   There are the regular X4 and X5 bus services travelling between Penrith and Keswick through Threlkeld (NY 325 253) and by Scales (White Horse Inn) (NY 342 268) which give good starting points to ascend Blencathra.

In 2024 there was no official bus stop at Scales and the buses did not always stop there for disembarking or embarking. I hope something can be resolved on this. See www.jaggedlakes.co.uk for any updates.

9   BLENCATHRA - continued

Phil Blanshard, Dave Hellier, John Howarth, Ron Kenyon, Andy Lloyd, Belinda Lloyd, Eric Parker, Ian Philips, Soo Redshaw and Mary Volume - 16/12/2023
213 down – and one to go - Blencathra!

We were looking for ascents by EVMC members up various routes. The weather forecast for Saturday 16th December looked the best and we arranged to meet using the 9.00am X5 bus from Sandgate, in Penrith, westward and Blencathra bound. Soo was in Cockermouth and boarded the X4 there and met us at Threlkeld. John just missed the 9.00am bus so caught the 10.15am bus and, being full of youth, bounded up after us. We split up for various routes as follows with:

Disembarking at Scales - Belinda and Eric going for Sharp Edge.
Mary heading to Scales Tarn and up left to the summit. Phil and Ian opting for Doddick Fell.

Disembarking at Threlkeld - Dave and Soo setting off up Hall's Fell.
Andy and Ron aiming for Middle Tongue.

Cloud had been gathering during the morning and the summit was covered in clouds but there was no rain and the south westerly wind was not as strong as was anticipated.

▲   Sharp Edge should not be underestimated. Luckily the wind was not too bad but the rock was quite wet and slippery and care was needed.

▲   **Blencathra** is one of the most trodden fells in the Lake District but the way up Middle Tongue, between Hall's Fell and Gategill Fell, is well away from the crowds. This starts up the valley, past various mine workings, then goes up the broad heathery tongue which leads eventually to the summit ridge.

Most of the team gathered on the summit and then set off towards Blease Fell to meet the Middle Tongue team, who then went on to the summit and met the late arriving John bounding along, having ascended Sharp Edge. A somewhat leisurely descent was then made back over Blease Fell and down to Threlkeld for welcome refreshment in the Salutation Inn to celebrate the completion of the 214 Wainwrights.

EVMC group on Blencathra on the completion of the Wainwrights (Walk **NF9**).

EVMC WAINWRIGHT CHALLENGE - SOUTHERN FELLS - 2023

1. **ROSTHWAITE FELL, GLARAMARA, ALLEN CRAGS and SEATHWAITE FELL**
   Robin Illingworth and Eric Parker - 20/01/2023

2. **GREEN CRAG, HARTER FELL and HARD KNOTT**
   Chris and Ron Kenyon - 19 - 11/05/2023

3. **LINGMELL**
   Chris and Ron Kenyon - 08/10/2023

4. **LANGDALE**
   (a) **COLD PIKE, CRINKLE CRAGS, BOWFELL, ESK PIKE and ROSSETT PIKE**
   (b) **PIKE O'BLISCO and LINGMOOR FELL**
   Chris and Ron Kenyon - 08 - 11/11/2023

5. **GREAT END, SCAFELL PIKE, SCAFELL, SLIGHT SIDE, ILLGILL HEAD and WHIN RIGG**
   Jane Meeks, Gary Baum and Rona - 21/11/2023

6. **CONISTON FELLS**
   (a) **BLACK CRAG and HOLME FELL**
   (b) **DOW CRAG, CONISTON OLD MAN, BRIM FELL, GREY FRIAR, GREAT CARRS and SWIRL HOW**
   (c) **WETHERLAM**
   Chris and Ron Kenyon - 26 - 29/11/2023

SOUTHERN FELLS

The Southern Fells stretch from the most southerly Wainwright summits of **Coniston Old Man**, **Wetherlam** and **Dow Crag** up to **Scafell**, **Scafell Pike**, **Great End**, **Bowfell** and **Crinkle Crags** in the Central Lakes and to the ridge of **Allen Crags**, **Glaramara** and **Rosthwaite Fell** stretching up into Borrowdale.

There are several passes crossing the area with Sty Head linking Borrowdale and Wasdale as well as Rossett Gill and Esk Hause across from Great Langdale to the top of Sty Head.

SOUTHERN FELLS

1 ROSTHWAITE FELL, GLARAMARA, ALLEN CRAGS and SEATHWAITE FELL

These fells are at the head of Borrowdale, encircling the valley of Grains Gill and leading up into the Central Fells from Seathwaite.
Glaramara overlooks the hanging valley of Combe Gill with **Rosthwaite Fell** to the east. The 'Wainwright' summit of **Rosthwaite Fell** is not Rosthwaite Cam at 612m but is **Bessyboot** at 551m, just next to Tarn at Leaves - it is recommended that one visits both summits! **Allen Crags** is further south, along the ridge from **Glaramara**, with the important central pass of Esk Hause nearby.
Seathwaite Fell is an extension of **Great End** and is towered over by the latter's impressive face.
Glaramara, **Allen Crags** and **Seathwaite Fell** were part of The Great Gift in 1924.

  There are various bus services up and down Borrowdale (77/77a or 78) and these can be used to access Stonethwaite (NY 257 142) and Seatoller (NY 246 137).

Robin Illingworth and Eric Parker - 20/01/2023
We took the bus via Keswick into Borrowdale, getting off at Stonethwaite, and ascended **Rosthwaite Fell**. Then we went along to **Glaramara** and **Allen Crags** before dropping down by Sprinkling Tarn to **Seathwaite Fell** and its summit at its north end. A rather steep descent took us onto Sty Head Pass from where we returned to Seathwaite and Seatoller and the bus back to Keswick.

From Allen Crags looking towards Pike o'Stickle (Walk **SF1**)
photo Rob Illingworth.

Opposite:

Above: View from Crinkle Crags to the Scafell Group (Walk **SF4**).

Below: Rosthwaite Fell (Bessyboot) and Tarn at Leaves (Walk **SF1**).

DETAILS AND TALES OF THE FELLS

2   GREEN CRAG, HARTER FELL and HARD KNOTT

Eskdale is a delightful valley and being on the west side of the Lake District, for many, it is more difficult to get to but much quieter (usually!) than other more accessible valleys.
These summits overlook the top end of the lower valley and, to the north, the upper River Esk leads into the Central Fells with **Scafell**, **Scafell Pike**, **Bowfell** and **Crinkle Crags**.

One of the big attractions of the valley is La'al Ratty - the Ravenglass and Eskdale Railway. This is a narrow gauge railway originally established for mining purposes but now a delightful tourist attraction and a useful means of transport up and down the valley. The head of the railway is at Dalegarth (SD 174 007) which is a great starting point for the fells beyond.

The La'al Ratty miniature railway links with the main Cumbria Coast Railway Line at Ravenglass (SD 087 964) .

There is no regular bus service in the Eskdale valley.

La'al Ratty (Northern Rock) making progress along Eskdale (Walk **SF2**).

Walking along the road in Eskdale from Boot to La'al Ratty (Walk **SF2**).

2 GREEN CRAG, HARTER FELL and HARD KNOTT - contd

Chris and Ron Kenyon - 09 – 11/05/2023

This was our first venture into the "far west". We caught the train to Carlisle and then the Cumbria Coast Railway Line to Ravenglass - not the fastest of journeys but interesting to see it go past Dalston, Wigton, Aspatria and Maryport. At Ravenglass we had to change from the "big train" to La'al Ratty and the River Irt locomotive arrived and was set up for the journey into Eskdale. The weather was excellent and we made our way to Dalegarth Station from where we walked up the valley road to the Woolpack Inn - a long established hostelry in Boot. It was mid-afternoon and we decided to have a look at Tortoise Crag, a newly developed crag, near Hare Crag and just beyond Wha House. We eventually found it and were pleased to find a slab of rock well up the fellside, with fine views of Upper Eskdale, with a selection of routes which very much suited Ron's style of climbing. On the way up to the crag we met a lady from Kendal who had her 20 month old daughter in a backpack and they had just been up **Slight Side** and **Scafell** - this was the 213th Wainwright for the little girl with only **Yewbarrow** still left to do. Her mum said she did her first Wainwright aged 2 months!

We met a group from London who were on a corporate challenge to climb **Scafell Pike** then Snowdon and were setting off at 6.00am the next day from Wasdale Head to climb **Scafell Pike**. They were presented with lightweight jackets in a dark green - surely, a bright and colourful jacket would have made more sense from a safety point of view. I'm not sure if they had a guide or a map but none seemed to have been up in the area before. We mentioned them to the hotel and it seems that a lot of people and organisations intending to climb **Scafell Pike** google **Scafell Pike** but just enter **Scafell** then look for a hotel and the Woolpack Inn comes up despite being in the wrong valley. So much for planning the route but it is good business for the Woolpack Inn.

Unfortunately the weather on the Wednesday was not so good but we set off via Doctor's Bridge, donning waterproofs, and climbed up by Birker Force and Low Birker Tarn, with views across to Yoadcastle and up to **Green Crag**. The amount of wear and tear on these paths is nothing like that on the more popular Lakeland fells and this was similar for the path across to **Harter Fell**, where we joined the "Grassguards path" to the summit and the short rock climb to attain the top, in thick mist. Continuing along the ridge we had some fine views, under the cloud, into the Upper Duddon valley, and arrived at the road at the top of Hardknott Pass. The previous weekend the Fred Whitton Cycle Challenge had passed this way and there was appropriate encouragement (Good Effort) painted on the road directed at the cyclists who had passed this way. Chris headed down the pass and Ron followed the path upwards to eventually reach the summit of **Hard Knott**. Sadly again no view! A bit of "off piste" took him along under Border End - the painter Heaton Cooper reckoned that the view from here into the Upper Esk was one of the best in the Lake District - but not today. Soon the valley and the Roman Fort came into view and he made his way back to and along the road for a welcome pint at the Woolpack Inn.

The weather was better on the Thursday and we made our way along the road to the station at Dalegarth for the 11.50am back to Ravenglass and the mainline train back to Penrith.

DETAILS AND TALES OF THE FELLS

3   LINGMELL

Lingmell is a delightful outlier of **Scafell Pike** but far fewer people will ascend this summit compared to its higher neighbour. It is however well worth considering climbing **Lingmell** at the same time as **Scafell Pike**. The south ridge which leads up from the **Scafell Pike** path, just above Brackenclose, is quite a slog but gives fine views down the valley and into the Scafells. **Lingmell** was part of The Great Gift in 1924.

Lingmell Col lies between **Lingmell** and **Scafell Pike** and is passed by the many ascending **Scafell Pike** but **Lingmell** summit can be gained by a short detour.

    The Wasdale Shuttle bus service operates during the summer.

    There is also access by foot over the passes of Burnmoor, Esk Hause and Sty Head into Wasdale.

Chris and Ron Kenyon - 08/10/2023
The day after Ron's ascent of **Kirk Fell** *and* **Pillar** *(see Walk* **WF 7***) dawned much better and from our overnight accommodation at the climbing hut at Wasdale Head, we could see folk heading "up the hill". There were various ways out of the valley such as over Burnmoor to Eskdale, La'al Ratty and train to Penrith or over Sty Head and back to Borrowdale.* **Lingmell** *loomed above and it seemed right to climb this on the way back to Borrowdale. Upward we went and it is quite an "up". We were followed by a group from the St Helens and District Ramblers' Group as the view over Wasdale and into the Scafells opened up. We met a couple of ladies and their dog, from Penrith, on the summit. Everyone in the area probably had* **Scafell Pike** *in their sights, however we went along the Corridor Route meeting lots of folk, heading upwards. They often made a comment such as "Are we nearly there yet?" to which we tried to reply in as optimistic way as possible. Eventually we reached Styhead Tarn and met with a friend and her new collie dog and we walked down with her. We parted company at Seathwaite and headed to the Glaramara Hotel, at Seatoller, and suitable refreshment before catching the 78 bus to Keswick. On the bus back to Penrith we were pleased to meet up with the Canadian chap whom we had met on the bus the day before and got to hear about his couple of days here before catching his 7.00pm train south from Penrith.*

Scafell Pike and Scafell from Lingmell (Walk **SF3**).

SOUTHERN FELLS

4   LINGMOOR FELL, PIKE O'BLISCO, COLD PIKE, CRINKLE CRAGS, BOWFELL, ESK PIKE and ROSSETT PIKE

The Great Langdale valley draws people in with the distinctive Langdale Pikes to the north and fine ridge of **Crinkle Crags** and **Bowfell** at its head.
Lingmoor Fell is on the south side of the valley with access either from the east end near Chapel Stile or from the road, near Blea Tarn, at the west end.
Pike o'Blisco overlooks Blea Tarn with access from the road nearby or from the top of Wrynose Pass.
Cold Pike, **Crinkle Crags** and **Bowfell** form a fine ridge between Langdale, Duddon Valley and Eskdale.
Esk Pike is next to Esk Hause which is the central link pass of the Lake District.
Rossett Pike separates Great Langdale from Langstrath and Borrowdale.

Orrest Head is close to the railway/bus station at Windermere. Although it is not a Wainwright, it has a special connection with AW in that it was the first summit attained by him, in 1930, and that first view of the Lakeland fells transformed his life and that of the many readers of his books.

There is the regular 516 bus service up the valley from Ambleside with links from Kendal, Windermere, Grasmere and Keswick.

There are a number of hotels and other accommodation in the valley together with the NT campsite at the head and a campsite at Chapel Stile along with a number of climbing club huts. There is a fine store in Chapel Stile for all provisions as well as Brambles Café.

Chris and Ron Kenyon - 08/11/2023 - 11/11/2023
A fine collection of summits was awaiting us in the Langdale valley and would necessitate staying over at a climbing hut. The forecast had looked good for Thursday and better for Friday and so on the Wednesday we boarded the train for Oxenholme and Windermere with a flexible plan. The bus and train times did not seem to interrelate with the hourly train arriving at 12.58pm and the hourly bus leaving at 12.54pm - why? We had taken an earlier train and had an hour to wait for the 516 bus service to Great Langdale. The autumn colours were shown off well in the sunshine as we sped along, through Ambleside, to disembark at our accommodation. After settling in, Chris went off for a walk and Ron set to with getting the coal fire going.
On the Thursday morning there was initial enthusiasm from Ron but reality struck and it was not a day for the Crinkles so the bus was taken to Ambleside to explore the village. Disembarking at Kelsick Road, the main bus stop, we paid visits to various shops then made our way to the Armitt Museum. After some food and more shop visiting we returned, on the 516 bus service, to the climbing hut where more people were taking up residence.

DETAILS AND TALES OF THE FELLS

4 (a) COLD PIKE, CRINKLE CRAGS, BOWFELL, ESK PIKE and ROSSETT PIKE

Ron Kenyon - 10/11/2023

On the Friday morning a big WOW was emitted when I looked through the curtains, at the clear skies. I was soon fed and watered and on the way at 7.30am heading along the road and **Cold Pike** bound. What a morning with a sprinkling of snow on the high summits! I met a cyclist heading along, who had just turned 60, and had set himself the challenge of going over by Blea Tarn then Wrynose and Hardknott passes to Brotherilkeld and back again! There was still mist over some of the fells which slowly dispersed. Turbocharged with my 600 kcal ration pack muesli, **Cold Pike** was soon attained then I continued onto **Crinkle Crags** - WHAT A DAY! The Bad Step, on the way up to the summit, is a bit tricky but can be avoided, if you want, to the left. The views all around were quite something!

Up in the snow I was making my way along and met a chap from Sussex who was heading towards **Great Gable** and looking to camp out overnight somewhere. We had a good chat as we made our way up **Bowfell**. Soon afterwards **Esk Pike** was in the bag - what a location, in the centre of the Lakes and on such a fine day! Going down from Ore Gap, I met Liam who comes from the Norfolk/Suffolk border and was also in the process of climbing all the Wainwrights without a car, in a year - a most impressive challenge given that he lives somewhat further away than the EVMC gang! He had been up in the Lakes, every month, travelling by train to get here and, with 41 summits left, he was looking to complete them all by the end of January - good luck Liam! On the way to **Rossett Pike** I met up with Pete and Andy, who were staying at the climbing hut, and we made our way down for a welcome pint at the Old Dungeon Ghyll (ODG).

Langdale Pikes from Lingmoor (Walk **SF4(b)**) - photo Chris Kenyon.

SOUTHERN FELLS

(b) PIKE O'BLISCO and LINGMOOR FELL

Chris Kenyon - 10/11/2023

*After Ron went off on his expedition I set off a bit later and walked up the valley to the Old Dungeon Ghyll and Stool End Farm. An amazing day with very clear, blue skies and some snow on the tops. I went up the steep path (thanks to Fix the Fells) to Red Tarn, then turned left up **Pike o'Blisco**. There are two cairns on the top so I went to both just to be certain of going to the higher. There were excellent views of **Crinkle Crags**, **Bowfell**, **Langdale Pikes** and further afield. I descended to Blea Tarn then decided whether I really wanted to go up **Lingmoor Fell**. The weather was still great so plodded my way to the top, then along the ridge and down to the Old Dungeon Ghyll just in time to catch the bus back to the climbing hut. A great day out!*

View from the summit of Pike o'Blisco to Crinkle Crags, Esk Pike and Bowfell.
(Walk **SF4(b)**) - *photo Chris Kenyon.*

4   ORREST HEAD - 11/11/2023

Job done! The day dawned equally as fine as the day before, and Chris set off with Pete and Andy, and made her way by the path at Harry's Place, over by **Silver How** *to Grasmere where she took the bus back home via Keswick. I took the bus back to the railway station at Windermere. On the bus I was chatting with a chap from Leeds who had camped overnight on* **Harrison Stickle** *(gobsmacking sky!) and he was getting the train back home. He had three hours to wait and I suddenly thought -* Orrest Head *- and mentioned that to him. This is a fine viewpoint close to the railway station and can be ascended quickly from there, and was a must for him (and me) that day.*

On the summit I met a couple from London, who had a 5-month old baby. This little one had a dislike of motor cars, so they had come north by train and were staying nearby with friends. There was a huge traffic jam on the road going to Ambleside and this couple had set off with the friends aiming for Little Langdale and had been stuck in that queue - little 5-month old did not like that! They had therefore come up Orrest Head *but also wanted to get to Ambleside and Little Langdale. I suggested using the steamer from Bowness-on-Windermere, which would avoid the queue, and they set off steamer bound whilst I went back to the railway station Penrith bound.*

View from Three Tarns, between Crinkle Crags and Bowfell, to the Scafell group (Walk **SF4(a)**).

SOUTHERN FELLS

5 GREAT END, SCAFELL PIKE, SCAFELL, SLIGHT SIDE, ILLGILL HEAD and WHIN RIGG

The **Scafells** and **Great End** overlook the head of the Wasdale valley and **Scafell Pike** (not **Scafell**) is (some say cursed as being) the highest summit in England and is a honeypot for walkers of a wide range of abilities. Sadly, the local Wasdale MRT is one of the busiest teams in the Lake District with, in amongst other rescues, helping many on their quests to conquer **Scafell Pike**. These are summits not to be taken lightly, especially by the inexperienced.
The summit of **Scafell Pike** and surrounding land was gifted to the National Trust by Lord Leconfield as a memorial to the men of the Lake District who fell in the Great War.
Great End was part of The Great Gift in 1924.
Scafell and **Slight Side** can be ascended from Wasdale Head but also can be ascended from Boot at the head of Eskdale.
On the north side of **Scafell** are the impressive rock buttresses of Scafell Crag and East Buttress, which complicate the access between **Scafell Pike** and **Scafell**.

End of a good long day with the sun setting over Wastwater (Walk **SF5**) - *photo Jane Meeks.*

5 GREAT END, SCAFELL PIKE, SCAFELL, SLIGHT SIDE, ILLGILL HEAD and WHIN RIGG - continued

▲ Broad Stand takes a line from near the south end of Mickledore towards the summit of Scafell and, over the years, has been the scene of fatal accidents and is best avoided. It should only be attempted by experienced scramblers and rock climbers and in dry conditions.
▲ Lord's Rake, to the right of Scafell Crag, is quite serious with loose rock in places.
▲ The route by Foxes Tarn, to the left of East Buttress is somewhat longer but safer.

When on the summit of **Scafell**, it is well worth making a slight diversion to the summit of Symonds Knott, just to the north of the main summit, for its fine view.
The Wasdale Screes are on the south side of Wastwater with the summits of **Ilgill Head** and **Whin Rigg**. These can be approached from Wasdale Head or Nether Wasdale as well as from Eskdale via Miterdale or Burnmoor Tarn.

Wasdale feels like, and indeed is, a remote valley, encircled by the highest fells in the Lake District with no easy access without a car. It is necessary to consider carefully the logistics of access to this area.

The Wasdale Shuttle bus service operates during the summer but only links with the main railway line, at Ravenglass, in the early morning and late afternoon.

Access by foot can be made by various ways including the passes of Sty Head from Borrowdale, Esk Hause from Langdale or Burnmoor from Eskdale.

Use of a bike would be useful, especially when the Shuttle Bus is not running.

Accommodation at the head of the valley includes the iconic Wasdale Head Inn as well as bed & breakfasts, two campsites and a climbing hut.

Jane, Gary and Rona - 21/11/23
An early start from near Penruddock, with two buses – the X5 bus service to Keswick, then the 78 bus service - got us to Seatoller by 9.15am. We then walked along the minor road to Seathwaite and took the path to Stockley Bridge and on up Grains Ghyll to **Great End**. The cloud was down on **Great End** but by **Scafell Pike** the sky had cleared and from then we had a magnificent day. We continued to **Scafell** via Lord's Rake. **Slight Side** followed and then Gary headed (limped) down towards the Wasdale Head Inn while the faster members of the party (Jane and German Shepherd Rona) went out-and-back to **Illgill Head** and **Whin Rigg**, then on to Wasdale Head Inn, to stay the night ready for **Yewbarrow** the next day (see Walk **WF9**).

Wasdale Head Inn
photo Jane Meeks.

SOUTHERN FELLS

6	**CONISTON FELLS**
(a)	**BLACK CRAG and HOLME FELL**
(b)	**DOW CRAG, CONISTON OLD MAN, BRIM FELL, GREY FRIAR, GREAT CARRS and SWIRL HOW**
(c)	**WETHERLAM**

The most southerly group of Lakeland fells encircles the Coppermines Valley, above the village of Coniston, with the summit of **Wetherlam** to the right, the main summit of **Coniston Old Man** to the left and the summit of **Dow Crag** above its impressive crags and rock climbing mecca to the south.

The rather lower **Black Crag** and **Holme Fell** may seem overshadowed by the nearby **Wetherlam** but are well worth ascending.

  There is the regular 505 bus service from Kendal/Windermere via Ambleside to Coniston. This bus service passes through Hawkshead and near **Black Crag**.

  There is also the bus service, run by Blueworks, from Barrow, via Ulverston to Coniston.

  There is a lot of accommodation including hotels, campsites and a climbing hut in the village, making it a great base for the area.

Chris and Ron Kenyon - 26 - 29/11/23
A nice collection of summits were waiting in the south of the Lake District and we planned on staying in a climbing hut in Coniston. The train took us via Oxenholme to Windermere station and then the 505 bus service continued via Ambleside to Coniston, with a short walk to the climbing hut. The term climbing hut understates the building and it is one of the oldest properties in the area, being built in 1654. We got the wood-burning stove into action and after a meal and a snug sleep got ready for the fells.

View from the popular Coniston Old Man (Walk **SF6(b)**).

DETAILS AND TALES OF THE FELLS

(a) BLACK CRAG and HOLME FELL

Chris and Ron Kenyon - 27/11/2023

We had planned on climbing the main Coniston Fells on this day however it dawned with a rather cloudy sky and an excellent forecast for the following day so we headed instead for these "outliers". We caught the 9.30am 505 bus and disembarked at High Cross (SD 333 987), just above Hawkshead Hill, where a pleasant road took us along to Knipe Fold with fine views towards Windermere and the prominent **Wansfell Pike***. Just before Knipe Fold a track leads up onto the fell, which eventually goes to Oxen Fell. The first summit was* **Black Crag** *gained by following a track through Iron Keld Plantation to its summit. Although relatively low it is away from the main fells and give one of the finest views in the Lake District - unfortunately today the clouds were down and that view could not be fully appreciated. Back to the main track we made our way along to the A593 road at Oxen Fell High Cross (NY 328 017).*

Holme Fell *overlooks the road to the west and we walked up the side road, leading to High Oxen Fell Farm, from where a track leads off left onto the fell. We made our way along the ridge with fine views in all directions. The main summit is at the south end of the ridge before it drops dramatically to Yewdale. From the summit we dropped back to the Uskdale Gap where a path drops down, above Yewdale Tarn, to the iconic High Yewdale farm. There is a good track and sign pointing to Coniston along the west side of the valley but we headed for the main road and path to Tarn Hows Cottage - we didn't think it was "up" - but up it was to this, again iconic, farmstead, before the track dropped back down, into the valley, along the Cumbria Way to Coniston.*

View from the summit of Black Crag towards Coniston (Walk **SF6(a)***).*

SOUTHERN FELLS

(b) DOW CRAG, CONISTON OLD MAN, BRIM FELL, GREY FRIAR, GREAT CARRS and SWIRL HOW

Ron Kenyon - 28/11/2023

The Coniston Fells tower above Coniston and give a mixture of routes with "The Old Man" being the honeypot summit. Today I had a few more to ascend so I set off at 8.00am. With a car one can avoid the initial climb by following a road to a car park at the end of the Walna Scar road and pay a fee for the pleasure of that. I took the main A593 road south to the small hamlet of Bowmanstead, and followed a path which ascends gently from there, to eventually join the Walna Scar track. The full blaze of the sunrise aided the climb as well as the views looking upwards towards the crags on **Dow Crag**. The Walna Scar track leads to a col, with the Duddon Valley beyond and from where the ridge is followed right to Brown Pike. As a slight variation I followed the old quarry road up to Blind Tarn, in an amazing classic glaciated corrie. The grassy slope, on the right, was then ascended (walking poles and / or fell running studs are recommended). On reaching the ridge, the **Scafells**, in the distance, came into view and the rest of the fells followed. Soon the rocky summit of **Dow Crag** was gained and some refreshment and more enjoyment of that view was had. More people were now about including the odd fell runner. There is a bit of a drop before the climb up to **Coniston Old Man** where I chatted to and took photos of various folk on the summit. When going along to **Brim Fell** my phone rang and it was Chris on **Wetherlam**, way off in the distance. A photo of **Wetherlam** summit was taken and zooming in confirmed she was on the summit. I was nearing the summit of **Brim Fell**, while on the phone. There were three ladies on the summit and I asked if we could all wave, which we did, and Chris could see our waves - simple pleasures of life! Onwards I went, down to the col of Levers Hause and just beyond that a path traverses leftward to a col and an ascent of **Grey Friar**. I realised that I don't get to this part of the Lake District often so had a prolonged stop for refreshment and appreciation of the surrounding fells. I headed back down to the col and then up **Great Carrs**, passing the wreckage and memorial to the crashed Halifax Bomber near the summit. **Swirl How** was my last summit that day, and the penultimate summit of the club's Wainwright Challenge. On the way down I went over Great Howe (a Birkett) to Levers Hause then down by Levers Water and the Pudding Stone. There are various ways down but I decided to go along to the car park at the Walna Scar Road then followed a track across and down, by Bowmanstead, to Coniston.

Extensive view from Dow Crag (Walk **SF6(b)**).

(c) WETHERLAM

Chris Kenyon - 28/11/2023

Ron set off on his longer walk and I left at about 8.30am. It was a cold sunny day and I walked up the road to the Coppermines Valley, passing various remains of the mining industry, then up to Red Dell valley. I went up by quite a faint path beside the stream then on up to the main ridge from where there was an amazing view - **Scafells**, **Great Gable**, **Crinkle Crags**, **Bowfell**, **Langdale Pikes** *- all clear and sharp in the sunshine. I continued up onto* **Wetherlam** *where I exchanged waves with Ron, across on* **Brim Fell**. *I went back down by Swirl Hause to Levers Water to the Coppermines Valley, where a walk back down the road took me into Coniston. A grand day out!*

Chris went back on the 505 bus service to Windermere and train to Penrith - Ron stayed on overnight and had some interesting chats in the pubs - but that is another story!

Early morning into the Coppermines Valley (Walk **SF6(b)**).

SOUTHERN FELLS

Above: Looking north from Holme Fell with a rainbow (Walk **SF6(a)**).

Below: View from Great Carrs towards the Scafell group with Hard Knott just in front and Seatallan and Haycock in the far distance (Walk **SF6(b)**).

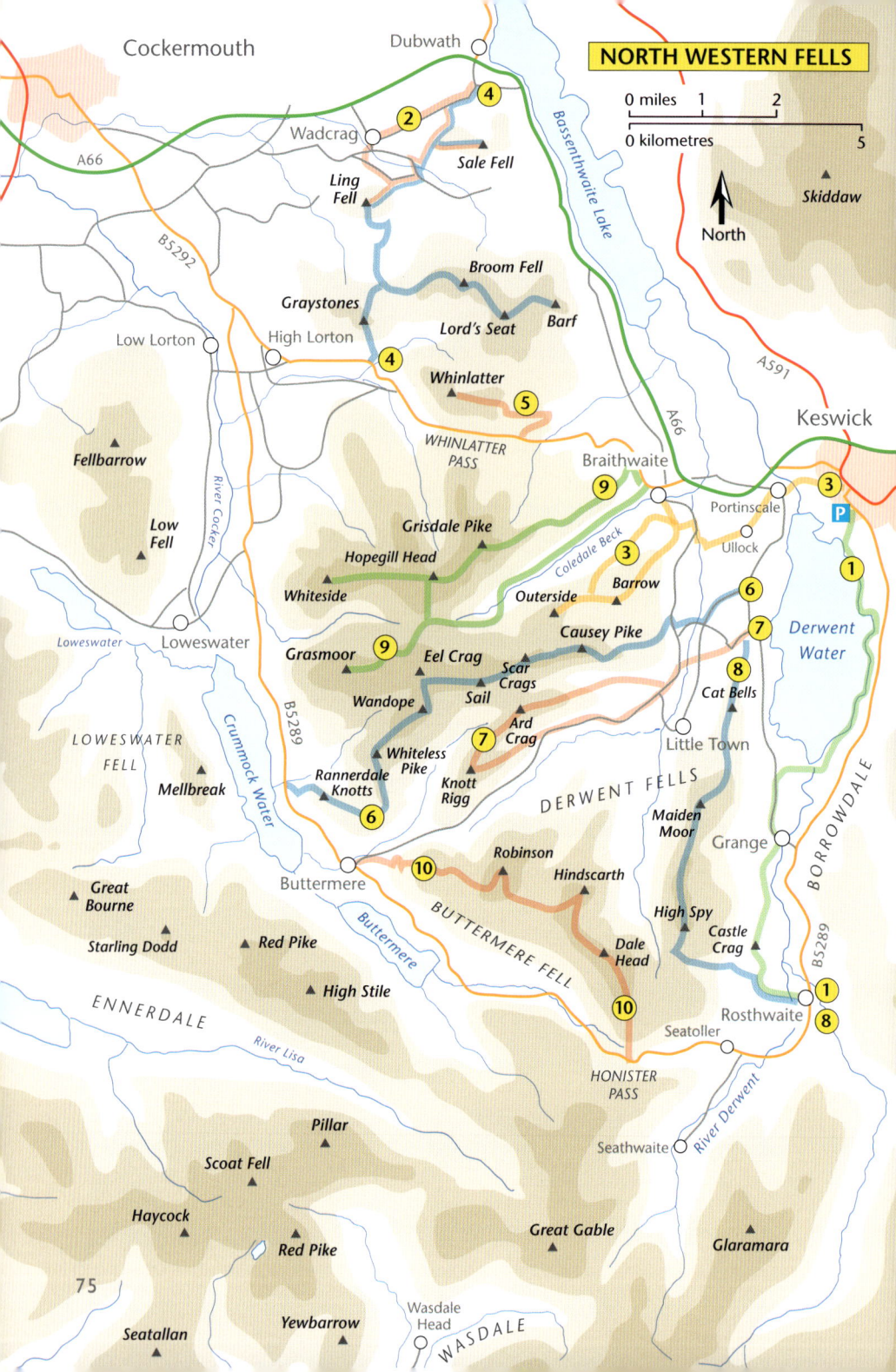

EVMC WAINWRIGHT CHALLENGE - NORTH WESTERN FELLS - 2023

1. **CASTLE CRAG**
   Chris Kenyon - 28/01/2023

2. **SALE FELL and LING FELL**
   Chris Kenyon - 06//02/2023

3. **BARROW and OUTERSIDE**
   Chris Kenyon - 17/02/2023

4. **SALE FELL, LING FELL, BROOM FELL, BARF, LORD'S SEAT and GRAYSTONES**
   Eric Parker - 03/03/2023

5. **WHINLATTER**
   Eric Parker - 07/03/2023

6. **RANNERDALE KNOTTS, WHITELESS PIKE, WANDOPE, EEL CRAG, SAIL, SCAR CRAGS and CAUSEY PIKE**
   Gary Newman and Ron Kenyon - 02/05/2023

7. **ARD CRAGS and KNOTT RIGG**
   Chris Kenyon - 01/06/2023

8. **CATBELLS, MAIDEN MOOR and HIGH SPY**
   Mary Volume - 28/07/2023

9. **GRISEDALE PIKE, HOPEGILL HEAD, WHITESIDE (there and back) and GRASMOOR**
   Jane Meeks, Gary Baum, Rona and Barney - 07/08/2023

10. **DALE HEAD, HINDSCARTH and ROBINSON**
    Mary Volume - 17/09/2023

NORTH WESTERN FELLS

The North Western Fells are to the west of Borrowdale, Keswick and Bassenthwaite Lake with the A66 and River Derwent along their eastern and northern sides and the valley of the River Cocker from Buttermere to Cockermouth to the west.

Honister Pass links Buttermere to Borrowdale on the southern side and Newlands Pass and Whinlatter Pass cross over the area. These roads divide the area with the fells of the Whinlatter area up to **Sale Fell** and **Ling Fell** in the north, the local "giants" of **Grasmoor**, **Whiteside**, **Hopegill Head** and **Grisedale Pike** leading along the classic ridge to **Causey Pike** in the middle and the long ridge of **Robinson**, **Dale Head**, **High Spy** to **Catbells** in the south and east.

View from Castle Crag towards Rosthwaite and Eagle Crag (Walk **NWF1**).

1   CASTLE CRAG

Castle Crag is located in the middle of Borrowdale, where it narrows, in the area known as the Jaws of Borrowdale. It is a very popular summit which can be accessed either from the village of Grange, to its north, or from Rosthwaite, to its south, by following the path along the side of the River Derwent. This can be done by various routes with both out-and-back or linear options. The summit is approached from its westerly side.

On the east side just above the path going along by the river are caves once lived in by Millican Dalton, the Professor of Adventure, in the 1930/40s and are worth hunting out.

The plaque on the summit highlights that the mountain was given to the National Trust by the Hamer Family in memory of John Hamer who was killed in action on 22 March 1918.

   There are the various bus services up and down Borrowdale (77/77a or 78) and these can be used to access Grange (NY 254 174) or Rosthwaite (NY 258 149).

Chris Kenyon - 28/01/2023
It was rather cloudy over the Lakes but I set off on "that bus" again to Keswick with **Castle Crag** *in my sights. A quick bus change in Keswick found me on the Borrowdale bus bound for Rosthwaite with the idea of a traverse of* **Castle Crag** *to Grange. I went through the village and along the path by the river. Just before* **Castle Crag** *I took the path which takes a more vertical form, away from the river path. This leads to a stile leading to a junction with a path from the other side and the final zigzags up through the old slate workings. The summit has a fine view down Borrowdale to Keswick and* **Skiddaw** *and also in the other direction into the central Lake District. The descent is initially back down the same way then below the north side and along the path beside the River Derwent and along to Grange. There is a bus stop on the east side of the bridge at Grange, however I just missed a bus and decided to make my way to Keswick on foot. First walking along the road, which goes on the west side of the lake, I then took the path branching right towards the lake, over the duckboards and the Chinese Bridge, to Lodore. There was the option to catch a bus or launch here but after a short section of the road past the Lodore Hotel, I followed a path on the right (east) side of the road, then by the lake near Barrow Bay to the road junction up to Wathendlath. I had thought of taking the path up to below Falcon Crag from the lay-by but it seemed too overgrown so I carried on by the road and Cockshot Wood and Friar's Crag to Keswick. I had made the most of the valley walk.*

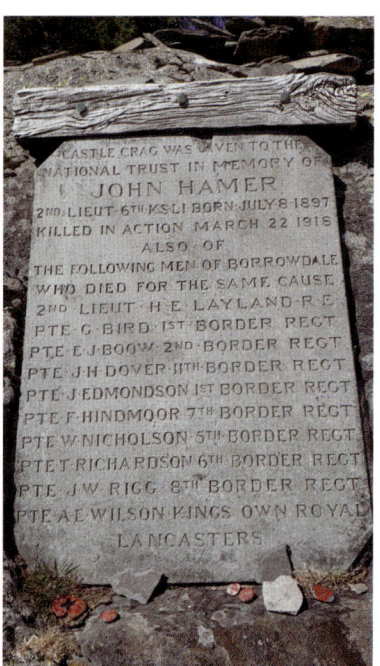

Memorial plaque on Castle Crag to the memory of John Hamer and the men of Borrowdale who died in WW1 (Walk **NWF1**).

DETAILS AND TALES OF THE FELLS

2   SALE FELL and LING FELL

These two fells are the most northerly on the west side of Bassenthwaite Lake with the fells around the Whinlatter Forest just to the south.

     The X5 (not the X4) bus service via Keswick to Workington goes up the west side of Bassenthwaite Lake and access to **Sale Fell** and/or **Ling Fell** is from the Pheasant Inn (NY 199 307) or Embleton (NY 175 304).

     The X4 bus service goes up the east side of Bassenthwaite Lake and through Embleton.

Chris Kenyon - 06/02/2023
I took the X5 bus service via Keswick to the Pheasant Inn, near Bassenthwaite Lake. I walked up along the road to below **Sale Fell**, *through a gate and up a gradual rising path, with good views, then more steeply to the summit. Then I headed back down into the pleasant Wythop Valley and across and up* **Ling Fell**. *I returned down to Wythop Mill and then back along the road to the Pheasant Inn.*

View from across the Wythop Valley to Lord's Seat with Skiddaw to the left and the Helvellyn Ridge in the distance (Walk **NWF2/4**).

NORTH WESTERN FELLS

3   BARROW and OUTERSIDE

Barrow and **Outerside** are on a subsidiary ridge, dropping down to Braithwaite, from the main ridge between **Eel Crag** and **Causey Pike**.

 The 77 bus service goes through Braithwaite (NY 231 236) and on over Whinlatter Pass by the Whinlatter Visitor Centre, between March and November.

 The X5 (not the X4) bus service also goes through Braithwaite (NY 231 236) and then along the west side of Bassenthwaite Lake.

Chris Kenyon - 17/02/2023
I caught the X5 bus via Keswick to Braithwaite - make sure you get the correct bus! I walked through the village and up **Barrow**, *where the top was clear, though the mist was swirling round the higher tops. On I went to* **Outerside**, *where I met two men coming down who warned me that the path was difficult and very slippery. I assured them that I would be very careful and continued to the top. The top was in mist but there was a rainbow further down the valley. The descent was over Stile End and back to Braithwaite, passing a lot of beautiful snowdrops in the woods. I decided to walk back, by Little Braithwaite, to Keswick, which was a pleasant walk through the fields.*
A good day out though modest by many people's standards.

View from Lord's Seat over Bassenthwaite Lake.

DETAILS AND TALES OF THE FELLS

4   SALE FELL, LING FELL, BROOM FELL, BARF, LORD'S SEAT and GRAYSTONES

These form most of the fells to the north of Whinlatter Pass. **Sale Fell** and **Ling Fell** look out over the A66 and the Solway Plain beyond with access from the north end of the Bassenthwaite Lake area. **Broom Fell**, **Lord's Seat**, **Barf** and **Graystones** are on the northern edge of Whinlatter Forest with access from the Whinlatter Pass or from Powter How, next to the A66, near Thornthwaite, up by The Bishop on **Barf.**

The 77 / 77a bus services go over Whinlatter, between March and November, and give access to the Whinlatter Forest area.

The X5 (not the X4) bus service between Penrith, via Keswick, to Workington goes up the west side of Bassenthwaite Lake and can give access to **Barf** from Powter How (NY 221 264) near Thornthwaite and to **Sale Fell** and **Ling Fell** from the Pheasant Inn (NY 199 307) or Embleton (NY 175 304).

The X4 bus service goes up the east side of Bassenthwaite Lake and through Embleton (NY 175 304) as well.

Eric Parker - 03/04/2023
I took the X5 bus service via Keswick to the Pheasant Inn, near the north end of Bassenthwaite Lake. **Sale Fell** *is just above and was gained by a circuitous route.* **Ling Fell** *is nearby, across the Wythop Valley, and followed by a route to* **Broom Fell**. **Barf** *is a bit of an outlier for this route then back over* **Lord's Seat**. **Graystones** *is the westerly outlier from which a descent, down to near Scawgill Quarry, led to the Whinlatter Pass and 77a bus service back to Keswick and home.*

Rock Sculpture on Barf.

NORTH WESTERN FELLS

5 WHINLATTER

Whinlatter is the fell along the north side of the road going over Whinlatter Pass and gives the area its name.

 The 77/77a bus services run between March and November from Keswick and go over Whinlatter Pass and may be used to take one to the Whinlatter Visitor Centre (NY 191 245).

Eric Parker   -   07/04/2023
This was to finish off the area following the visit four days earlier. I took the bus to Keswick then the 77 bus service to the Whinlatter Visitor Centre. From here, there are various routes around the forest and I followed one of these to the top of **Whinlatter** *and came back the same way.*

77A bus at the Whinlatter Forest Visitor Centre.

Panoramic view from the summit of Whinlatter showing Skiddaw, the Pennines in the distance, Clough Head to Helvellyn and Grisedale Pike (Walk **NWF5**).

6   RANNERDALE KNOTTS, WHITELESS PIKE, WANDOPE, EEL CRAG, SAIL, SCAR CRAGS and CAUSEY PIKE

These form a combination of summits which can be traversed in this way or as part of a horseshoe and linked to other summits.

Rannerdale Knotts is right next to the road, by Crummock Water, and can easily be ascended on its own. Rannerdale, to its north, is well known for its bluebells in the summer and is also "The Secret Valley" in the book of that name by Nicholas Size taking us back 1,000 years to Norman times.

Above **Rannerdale Knotts**, **Whiteless Pike** and **Wandope** are on the ridge on the side of **Eel Crag** and can be linked to **Grasmoor**, returning by Lad Howes ridge.

Eel Crag (also known as Crag Hill), **Sail**, **Scar Crags** and **Causey Pike** are on the stunning ridge running eastwards from **Eel Crag**, down to Newlands valley.

   The 77 and 77a bus services encircle these fells giving access, between March and November, at various locations: Rannerdale (NY 163 183), Buttermere village (NY 174 169) and near the Swinside Inn (NY 245 218) as well as the top of Whinlatter Pass (NY 191 245) and Braithwaite (NY 231 236).

   The area can be accessed by the 77c bus service between Cockermouth and Buttermere.

Gary Newman and Ron Kenyon - 02/05/2023
We caught the bus to Keswick and then the 77 bus service over Whinlatter Pass to Lorton and disembarked below **Rannerdale Knotts**. *Another couple were setting off to look at the bluebells and then aiming for Braithwaite.*
On the summit of **Rannerdale Knotts** *we saw local artist Alan Roper, from Maryport, working away at a sketch of the summit rocks. We headed on along the ridge then upward towards the summit of* **Whiteless Pike,** *for a bite to eat, followed by Whiteless Edge to* **Wandope**. *We had intended to climb* **Grasmoor** *but time was limited to catch the bus so we decided to continue to* **Eel Crag**. *On* **Sail** *we met a chap and his wife, with his son and friend. He had just retired and was having three months in the Lake District ticking away at the Wainwrights. On downwards over* **Scar Crags**, *we met a lady leading an HF group - she had 25 Wainwrights to do and was looking forward to getting into the Western Lakes soon.* **Causey Pike** *came and went and we headed down to the Newlands Valley and the Swinside Inn, for a welcome pint before catching the 77 bus, which passed nearby, back to Keswick.*

NORTH WESTERN FELLS

Above: Alan Roper in action on the summit of Rannerdale Knotts with a copy of the drawing as well as a painting by him of Rannerdale Knotts, Crummock Water and Red Pike/High Stile beyond (**NWF6**).

Above: Gary Newman making his way along to Scar Crags and Causey Pike with Skiddaw, Blencathra and Clough Head in the distance (Walk **NWF6**).

Left: A busy time on the summit of Sail (**NWF6**).

DETAILS AND TALES OF THE FELLS

7   ARD CRAGS and KNOTT RIGG

These two fells are on an outlier ridge from **Robinson** and can be approached from the road at the top of Newlands Pass. Without a car there is a bit of a walk to get to the fells either from the Newlands Valley or from Buttermere village.

 The 77/77a bus service encircles the area and can be used for access to Braithwaite (NY 231 236), for Newlands Valley, or Buttermere village (NY 174 169).

 The Derwentwater launch gives access to the Newlands Valley via Hawse End (NY 247 212).

 The area can be accessed by the 77c bus service between Cockermouth and Buttermere.

Chris Kenyon - 01/06/2023
I took the bus to a busy Keswick then the launch across to Hawse End. I left the hordes going up **Catbells** *and took the pleasant field paths to the Newlands Valley road and to the bottom of* **Ard Crags***. I incorrectly followed a vague path which ended in a dead end – so went up the bank to the proper path! After ascending* **Ard Crags***, I continued along to* **Knott Rigg***. With lovely views, I carried on down the ridge, to Keskadale Farm then along the road/path to Braithwaite and the bus home.*

Signs near Swinside Inn *(Walk* **NW6***)*.

NORTH WESTERN FELLS

8   CATBELLS, MAIDEN MOOR and HIGH SPY

Catbells is one of the most trodden fells in the Lake District with easy access and fine views over Derwentwater. The ridge going south makes a fine outing with **Maiden Moor** and **High Spy**, before dropping down to Rosthwaite. Doing the walk in the other direction will give the pleasure of looking at the **Catbells** ridge, with Derwentwater and **Skiddaw** in the background. **Catbells** can be climbed on its own with a combination of a walk by the lake, buses and/or a launch.

    There are the 77 and 77a bus services (March – November) from Keswick to Buttermere (the 77a is clockwise and at first goes past **Catbells**).

    There is the 78 bus service going up and down Borrowdale.

    There are the launches on Derwentwater with various stops (Hawse End, Brandelhow) on the side of **Catbells** and it is great to incorporate a ride on a boat with a walk.

Mary Volume - 28/07/2023
I went out today and up **Catbells**, **Maiden Moor** *and* **High Spy**. *From Keswick I took the 77A bus to the north end of the* **Catbells** *ridge over* **Maiden Moor** *and* **High Spy** *and then dropped down to Rosthwaite and went back to Keswick on the 78 bus.*

Catbells and Maiden Moor with Skiddaw and Blencathra in the distance (Walk **NWF8**).

144

DETAILS AND TALES OF THE FELLS

9   GRISEDALE PIKE, HOPEGILL HEAD, WHITESIDE and GRASMOOR

These are the fine summits in the central area of the North Western Fells.
Grisedale Pike, **Hopegill Head** and **Whiteside** form a ridge along the north side of the area with the large bulk of **Grasmoor** off to the south.

    The 77 and 77a bus services encircle the area giving access at numerous points for these fells.

    The area can be accessed by the 77c bus service between Cockermouth and Buttermere.

    On the east side of the area, Braithwaite (NY 231 236) is a useful access point.

    On the north side, Whinlatter Pass at The Visitor Centre (NY 191 245) gives a higher access point.

    On the south side, Lanthwaite Green (NY 158 208) and the road by Crummock Water to Buttermere village (NY 163 194) give access to the rather daunting-looking south faces of Whiteside and Grasmoor.

Jane Meeks, Gary Baum, Rona and Barney - 07/08/2023

A 25 minute walk through wet grass got us from home to the recently reopened Herdwick Inn, in Penruddock, from where the X5 bus service took us to Braithwaite. We then had a lovely outing over **Grisedale Pike, Hopegill Head** and **Whiteside** out-and-back) and then **Grasmoor**. We descended past the Force Crag mines and the associated waterfalls that always bring back memories of possibly the most fun Lakeland ice climb I've done. After a vegan scone in the excellent Jasper's Café in Braithwaite, a rather full X5 bus returned us to Penruddock after what turned out to be a good day out.

Hopegill Head and Grasmoor from the path to Grisedale Pike from Whinlatter (Walk **WL9**).

NORTH WESTERN FELLS

10   DALE HEAD, HINDSCARTH and ROBINSON

These summits overlook the north side of Honister Pass forming a fine ridge with a possible link to **High Spy** and along to **Catbells**.

The 77a (clockwise) and 77 (clockwise) bus services go over Honister Pass (between March and November) and give the easiest way to start at the top of the pass (NY 225 135). There are bus stops at a number of points including Rosthwaite (NY 258 149) and Buttermere village (NY 174 169).

The area can be accessed by the 77c bus service between Cockermouth and Buttermere.

Mary Volume - 17/09/2023
This is the fine ridge, just to the north of Honister Pass, between Buttermere and Newlands Valley. I made use of the 77a bus service, from Keswick, to gain height to the top of Honister Pass. From there I ascended **Dale Head** *then went along the fine ridge over* **Hindscarth** *and* **Robinson** *before descending (not good on knees) to Buttermere and the bus back to Keswick.*

View north-east from Dale Head with the High Spy to Catbells ridge, Blencathra, Clough Head to Helvellyn Ridge and the Pennines in the far distance (Walk **NWF10**).

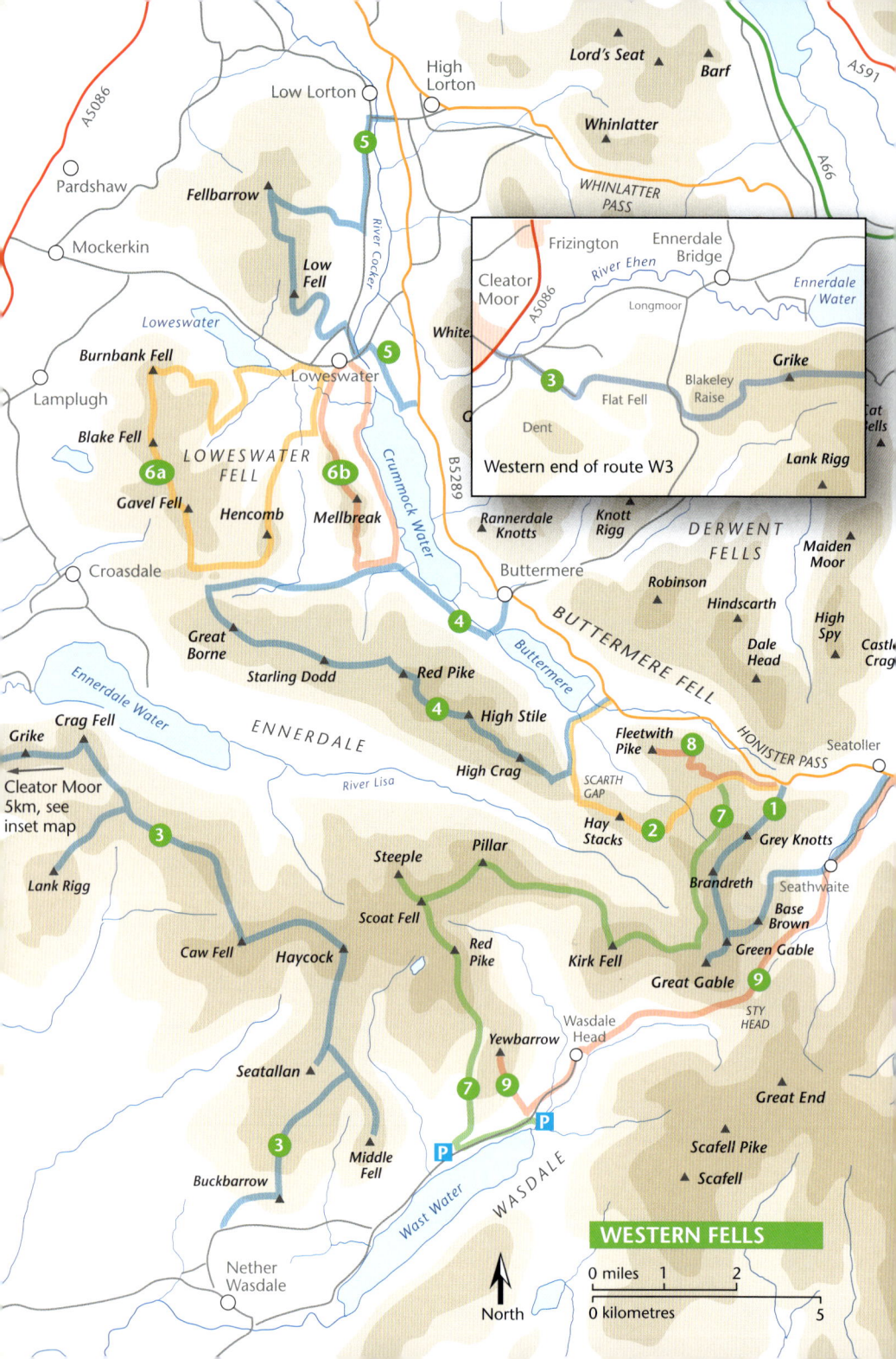

EVMC WAINWRIGHT CHALLENGE - WESTERN FELLS - 2023

1. **BASE BROWN, GREEN GABLE, GREAT GABLE, BRANDRETH and GREY KNOTTS**
   Eric Parker - 20/04/2023

2. **HAYSTACKS**
   Mary Volume - 28//04/2023

3. **GRIKE, CRAG FELL, LANK RIGG, CAW FELL, HAYCOCK, SEATALLAN, MIDDLE FELL and BUCKBARROW**
   Ron Kenyon - 07 - 09/07/2023

4. **GREAT BORNE, STARLING DODD, RED PIKE (Buttermere), HIGH STILE and HIGH CRAG**
   Ron Kenyon - 03/09/2023

5. **FELLBARROW and LOW FELL**
   Ron Kenyon - 14/09/2023

6. (A) **BURNBANK FELL, BLAKE FELL, GAVEL PIKE and HEN COMB**
   (B) **MELLBREAK**

   Chris and Ron Kenyon - 21 - 22 /09/2023

7. **KIRK FELL, PILLAR, STEEPLE, SCOAT FELL and RED PIKE (Wasdale)**
   Ron Kenyon - 07/10/2023

8. **FLEETWITH PIKE**
   Chris and Ron Kenyon - 2710/2023

9. **YEWBARROW**
   Jane Meeks, Gary Baum and Rona - 21/11/2023

WESTERN FELLS

This is the large area of land between the Buttermere valley to the north and Wasdale to the south. It is bisected by the Ennerdale valley which is encircled by the fells of the Ennerdale Horseshoe with **Great Borne**, **Red Pike**, **High Stile**, **Haystacks**, **Great Gable**, **Kirk Fell**, **Pillar** and **Haycock** and the other fells falling away from this central mass.

Rock climbers in action on the route Oxford and Cambridge Climb, on Grey Crag, with a view to Fleetwith Pike and Robinson beyond (Walk **WF4**).

WESTERN FELLS

1   BASE BROWN, GREEN GABLE, GREAT GABLE, BRANDRETH and GREY KNOTTS

These summits are to the west side of the head of Borrowdale, near Seathwaite.
They were part of the Great Gift of the FRCC in 1924 with the main summit of **Great Gable** looking down over Wasdale and across to the **Scafells**.
When on **Great Gable**, it is well worth going to Westmorland Cairn, which is just south-west of the main summit and above Westmorland Crag, to enjoy the stunning view over Wasdale. There are fine views from all the summits looking in all directions but especially westwards into the Ennerdale and Buttermere valleys.

These summits can be approached from the north, from Keswick, by using the 78 bus service to Seatoller (NY 246 137) or the 77/77a bus services to the summit of Honister Pass (NY 225 135), between March and November.

The area can be accessed by the 77c bus service between Cockermouth and Buttermere.

Eric Parker - 20/04/2023
I had a good day today with the buses working like a dream! After taking the 7.50am X4 bus service from Penrith to Keswick, I had about 5 minutes to wait in Keswick for the 78 bus service to Seatoller. After walking along to Seathwaite I ascended by Sour Milk Gill then up **Base Brown**, **Green Gable** *to* **Great Gable**. *Retracing my steps over* **Green Gable** *I finished over* **Brandreth** *and* **Grey Knotts**. *I arrived at the top of Honister Pass at 2.05pm and the bus arrived two minutes later. I got back into Keswick just as the Penrith bus pulled in and I was back in Penrith just after 4.00pm.*

View from Brandreth over Buttermere with High Stile, Mellbreak and Grasmoor (Walk **WF1**).

150

2 HAYSTACKS

This was AW's favourite fell and where his ashes were laid. It can be accessed from Gatesgarth Farm, next to Buttermere, as part of a traverse of the ridge between Buttermere and Ennerdale or else from the top of Honister Pass.

 The 77/77a bus services from Keswick go by Buttermere village (NY 174 169), Gatesgarth (NY 194 149) and Honister Pass (NY 225 135) between March and November.

 The area can be accessed by the 77c bus service between Cockermouth and Buttermere.

Mary Volume - 28/04/2023
I took the bus to Keswick and then the 77a bus service onto Gatesgarth Farm, next to Buttermere. I walked up to Scarth Gap then up to the summit of **Haystacks** *and onwards. I was amazed at the number of paths around the place. I was looking to go to the top of Honister Pass to benefit from the easier descent, rather than going back to Gatesgarth Farm. I had* **Fleetwith Pike** *in mind as well, however its inclusion could have meant missing the bus back to Keswick, so I just went straight to Honister Pass and caught the bus back to Keswick and Penrith.*

Haystacks with Great Gable beyond *(Walk* **WF2***)*.

WESTERN FELLS

3   GRIKE, CRAG FELL, LANK RIGG, CAW FELL, HAYCOCK, SEATALLAN, MIDDLE FELL and BUCKBARROW

The area between Wasdale and Ennerdale broadens out around the valley of the River Bleng which flows down through Gosforth and is encircled by these fells.

The far Western Fells are not too well serviced by public transport but the crucial link is the number 30 bus service from Whitehaven to Cleator Moor (NY 027 145).

The Wasdale Shuttle bus is a welcome service up and down Wasdale, in the summer, between Nether Wasdale and Wasdale Head during the day, and via Ravenglass at the beginning and end of the day.

The area can be accessed by the 77c bus service between Cockermouth and Buttermere.

Ron Kenyon - 07 - 09/07/2023
The fells on the west of the Lakes, to the north of Wasdale, are particularly difficult to access by bus. Cleator Moor was the key. I took the train and the Cumbria Coast Railway Line from Carlisle to Whitehaven and then the 30 bus service to Cleator Moor, which weaved its way through the outskirts of Whitehaven and Cleator Moor to the junction with the A5086. Then I followed the road over Wath Bridge and up Nannycatch Road, by the White House, and onto the fell (in fact Flat Fell) following a track to the Kinniside stone circle where I met a couple, setting out on a Wainwright quest.
Blakeley Raise (a Birkett) led to **Grike** *and then* **Crag Fell** *with* **Lank Rigg** *looking somewhat distant. Dropping off my rucksack, before Whoap, aided the out-and-back to* **Lank Rigg** *then I headed over Ennerdale Fell (another Birkett) to* **Caw Fell** *and got a glimpse of the grand views up Ennerdale and of the* **Scafells**. *I went past Little Gowder Crag (another Birkett) to the grand-looking* **Haycock** *with its views in all directions.*

Summit of Seatallen with the Scafell group in the distance (Walk **WF3**).

3 GRIKE, CRAG FELL, LANK RIGG, CAW FELL, HAYCOCK, SEATALLAN, MIDDLE FELL and BUCKBARROW - continued

It was all "downhill" from here - well not quite! I had a tent and had thought that I might reach Nether Wasdale (and the pub) or Greendale Tarn but the time was ticking on. I passed some small pools in a grand setting for a camp and with the time at 5.30pm decided this was the place for the night - and what a place! The tent was soon up and I was installed with a cup of tea, a rehydrated evening meal and Jim Crumley's book 'Lakeland Wild' - and then the sunset and that view across to the **Scafells** with **Seatallan** waiting there for me in the morning.

The next day, after decamping, I dumped my rucksack part way up **Seatallan** and plodded up to the fine summit and view. On the way down I met a couple of ladies (from Aspatria and Penrith) on their way (remember this was 9.00am) and I asked where they had been. They had been anticipating a storm later in the day and had set off at 5.00am and had climbed **Middle Fell** and **Haycock** and go off down by **Buckbarrow** - the storm did come later but 5.00am was a bit early - but good planning!

I returned to the rucksack and went on to **Middle Fell** with a pleasant ascent (without a rucksack) then came back to contour above Greendale Tarn to Glade How (another Birkett). I actually had a telephone call, at this point, from another Birkett - Bill's nephew, Dave Birkett - on a rock climbing matter. Then it was down to **Buckbarrow** and after a quick look at the Upper Section of Pikes Crag I headed down to the road.

The time was 12.30pm and the issue now was to get to the railway without a car. One way was to walk to Murthwaite Station to catch the La'al Ratty but my legs did not feel like that. The Wasdale Shuttle bus went between Nether Wasdale and Wasdale Head, during the day, then to Ravenglass for the last trip (4.45pm or 6.15pm). So I thought why not go up the valley to the "fleshpots" of Wasdale Head with the Inn and the Barn Door climbing shop to while away the time (as well as some liquid and food refreshment and watch Wimbledon on the television). Under the "Laws of Sod" I expected to see the bus go past as I approached the road but it arrived about 3 minutes after – so on I got and headed for the head of the valley.

It was also the day of the Wasdale Fell race with runners spread around the fell tops.

At Wasdale Head there was the usual group of people with "that summit" as their only goal. I was approached and asked if I had been "Up" - I asked "Up what?" and they seemed confused. Eventually I realised it was "that summit" and pointed out where to go - they seemed quite reasonable folk but not fully aware of where "that summit" was or what an ascent entailed.

It was quite a pleasant, though close, day and the bad weather held off but that anticipated storm hit Wasdale at about 4.35pm - 10 minutes before the bus arrived! It also hit Grasmere a little time later as Chris found out - see Walk **CF9**. Ravenglass bound, I could sit back and hope for a train back home. Unfortunately weekend trains on the Cumbrian Coast Line are a bit limited and I ended up camping at the campsite near the village. It is owned by the Pennington family of Muncaster Castle and it was delightful. I had a pleasant evening in the Inn at Ravenglass which had a good range of music (care of Spotify) - much from my era!

A vanilla dessert and a cup of tea was an initial breakfast with a bacon butty later at La'al Ratty Café then I took the 10.36am train back via Carlisle. I had an interesting chat with a chap about killing of foxes and also the Black Panther, which he had seen in the south of the County - you never know what you will learn about!

WESTERN FELLS

4   GREAT BORNE, STARLING DODD, RED PIKE (Buttermere), HIGH STILE and HIGH CRAG

These fells are on the south side of Buttermere and Crummock Water and provide a bit of a challenge. It is possible to access them in sections but the whole ridge (and could include **Haystacks** and **Fleetwith Pike** as well) gives a great day out.

   Access from Buttermere village (NY 174 169) is the most appropriate way with use of the 77/77a bus services, between March and November.

   Access from the south side, in the Ennerdale valley, is rather limited without a car though a bike helps to open up possibilities.

   The area can be accessed by the 77c bus service between Cockermouth and Buttermere.

Ron Kenyon - 03/09/2023
There was a climbing club committee meeting in Buttermere at the start of September so it seemed a good chance to get the bus over there, stay overnight at the club hut and get away early in the morning. I took the usual X5 bus to Keswick. There were three Eden Runners on the bus going to participate in a trail race in the Northern Fells. It was then onward on the 77 bus over Whinlatter to the Buttermere valley. There was some confusion at the junction left to Crummock Water, where there was a diversion sign, which distracted the bus driver and he mistakenly went right and we headed for Loweswater - luckily a large turning point turned up and the driver could turn the bus round!
Up at just after 6.00am I was off at about 7.00am with a few folk about making the most of the glorious morning. I went by Scales Force and Floutern Tarn to the first summit of **Great Borne** with the ridge leading eastwards. It was not quite as clear as expected but it was not a bad view along the ridge. **Starling Dodd** led on to **Red Pike** where I could see the Beacon Pike, the hill above Penrith. At **High Stile** I had a look at Grey Crag, in Birkness Combe, and saw the Woodbury family, from Cockermouth, climbing the classic rock climb Oxford and Cambridge Direct. I followed the ridge to **High Crag** then downward to where I met various folk flogging up **High Crag**. Quite low down I met a group of three, not overly prepared, going off to a plunge pool which seemed to be in Warnscale Beck - they seemed quite undaunted (or more likely unknowing) to approach via **Haystacks**.
I had high expectations of an ice cream and/or a cup of tea at Gatesgarth - but the café was closed! I headed back to the climbing hut for a cup of tea then caught the 5.20pm bus back to Keswick - with a bit of an extreme bus ride down from Honister!

Road sign near Kirkstile (Walk **WF5**).

DETAILS AND TALES OF THE FELLS

5   FELLBARROW and LOW FELL

These two summits are located between Lorton and Loweswater, being outliers to the other fells in this area and give stunning views into the Buttermere valley and also out towards the Solway Firth and Scotland in the distance.

    The summits are accessed using the 77/77a bus services between March and November. There are crossing points of the River Cocker at Low Lorton and Scale Hill with bus stops being at Low Lorton (NY 153 257) and Lanthwaite Green (NY 158 208).

    The area can be accessed by the 77c bus service between Cockermouth and Buttermere.

Ron Kenyon - 14/09/2023
I caught the 9.15am X5 bus to Keswick. At the bus station at Sandgate in Penrith I met a couple from Brisbane, who were in England for 5 weeks. They were off to Keswick but only had one hour before catching the bus back, then off to Huddersfield - busy schedule!
On the 77 (anti-clockwise) bus to Buttermere I sat next to a chap from Keswick, with a B&B business, who was on his eighth Wainwright Round and had done the Birketts twice! As a variation on the Wainwrights, he was doing them in alphabetical order and in reverse - i.e. starting with **Yoke**. Today, amongst others, he was including two summits - **Whiteside** then **Whiteless Pike** - and in that order.
I disembarked at Low Lorton and followed the road along through Littlethwaite to Thackthwaite (a delightful hamlet) then headed up the path onto the fell. I met a lady from Dusseldorf who comes over frequently with her dog, a briard, which is a breed, originally from France, used for herding sheep - so it showed interest in sheep but no other animals.
I continued onto the rather rounded summit of **Fellbarrow** then along by Watching Crag (well named - great viewpoint) to **Low Fell.** This area is now a nature reserve with land acquired by Buy Land Plant Trees CIC. From the subsidiary summit of Lowthwaite Fell there is a great view across to the fells to the south of Loweswater as well as up the Buttermere valley. There was a rather awkward and not too obvious descent then by Whinny Ridding and Netherclose to Scalehill Close (sadly no time for drink at the Kirkstile Inn). From the bridge I went through Lanthwaite Wood to catch the bus at Lanthwaite Green.

View from Lowthwaite Fell.

155

WESTERN FELLS

6   MELLBREAK, BURNBANKS, BLAKE FELL, GAVEL PIKE and HEN COMB

These are the fells to the south of Crummock Water and Loweswater which overlook Ennerdale to the south. **Mellbreak** is feasible from Buttermere village (NY 174 169) but the others are best ascended from the Kirkstile area, to the east of Loweswater, and accessed from the bus stop at Lanthwaite Green (NY 158 208). The fells could be done in one day using the first and last buses or you could stay overnight in the area.

   The area can be accessed by the 77 or 77a bus loop from Keswick to Buttermere between March and November.

   The area can be accessed by the 77c bus service between Cockermouth and Buttermere.

Chris and Ron Kenyon - 21 - 22/09/2023
We decided to have a night at the Kirkstile Inn to aid access to the area. As usual, we took the X5 bus to Keswick and the 77 (anti-clockwise) bus over Whinlatter Pass and disembarked at Lanthwaite Green. We then took the track from Lanthwaite Gate to Scalehill Bridge and followed the road to the Kirkstile Inn, leaving spare clothing there.

View across Crummock Water to Rannerdale Knotts (Walk **WF6(b)**) - *photo Chris Kenyon.*

156

6(a) BURNBANK FELL, BLAKE FELL, GAVEL PIKE and HEN COMB

Ron Kenyon - 21/09/2023

I headed off and along the road to Maggie's Bridge, then by Loweswater, to Watergate Farm, where I chatted to the National Trust chap there (it is a National Trust property). I mentioned access to **Burnbanks** and he said there was forestry work and the track up, through the wood, was closed. So it was along to High Nook Farm, up the valley and along the side of Carling Dodd, where I met a group of local ladies who were part of the local "Walk 4 Fun" group. Further on I met another lady from Frizington with four lively and friendly dogs before making a "direct attack" on **Burnbanks** for the fine view over to Scotland and the Isle of Man. On the summit there were a couple who had been over **Hen Comb** and warned me of the river crossing point below Little Dodd. **Blake Fell** seemed to loom above but I plodded on to enjoy the fine view in all directions from its summit. I continued over **Gavel Pike** and the boggy wastes of Whiteoak Moss, where the Fix the Fells had had rocks helicoptered in to start improvements on the path. On **Hen Comb**, with its views into the Buttermere valley, I pondered on dropping down and along Mosedale but the Birkett summit of Little Dodd drew me down along the ridge. At the crossing point of the river some of the stepping stones were under water but with the aid of walking poles the river was soon crossed and the way along to the Kirkstile Inn enjoyed.

Ladies from the local *Walk 4 Fun* Club above Loweswater (Walk **WF6(a)**).

WESTERN FELLS

6(b)   MELLBREAK

Chris Kenyon - 21/09/2023
I had a coffee at the Kirkstile Inn after Ron went off summit-bagging, then went up the north ridge of **Mellbreak**. *This had an unpleasant patch of scree in the middle section but then it improved on the way up to the first top (508m). Great views! Onward I walked to the col and up to the main summit (512m) and then went down the south slope and round to the lakeshore of Crummock Water. I thought this might be really boggy after recent rain but it was fine. So far I had seen two people and a few in the distance though it was a bit busier by the lakeshore. The views across the lake and up Buttermere valley were lovely. I then headed back to the Kirkstile Inn (not quite by the route intended). After rain in the morning the weather in the afternoon was clear and sunny and I managed to do the whole walk without getting wet feet.*

The following morning we were greeted with heavy squally showers! There was a bus from Lanthwaite Green at 11.03am so we gave ourselves an hour to work our way over there. We took the road to the lake and at Park Bridge followed the path along to and by the lakeshore, passing the pump house, over bridges and the fish ladder to Lanthwaite Wood and back again to Lanthwaite Green to await the bus. On the bus we sat behind two ladies from southern China who were staying in Keswick and getting the most of the 77 (anticlockwise) bus route and they disembarked, above Hawse End, for an ascent of Catbells. Back in Keswick we just missed the Penrith bus so after a quick visit into town we had lunch at Booths before the next bus home - we seemed to have put a lot into the short time away!

View along the summit ridge of Mellbreak (Walk **WF6(b)**) - *photo Chris Kenyon.*

DETAILS AND TALES OF THE FELLS

7   KIRK FELL, PILLAR, STEEPLE, SCOAT FELL and RED PIKE (Wasdale)

These fells are between the valleys of Wasdale and Ennerdale and are somewhat remote, being especially inaccessible by bus. **Pillar** stands aloft in this area and, with Pillar Rock, towers above on the ridge along the southern side of Ennerdale. Nearby **Scoat Fell** has the rather impressive **Steeple** dropping off to its north and **Red Pike** to its south.

At the head of Wasdale, **Kirk Fell** is like a brother to **Great Gable** looking down over the valley. Both these fells were part of The Great Gift in 1924.

   Wasdale is a stunning valley and has the Wasdale Shuttle bus service during the summer but nothing at other times of the year.

   For Ennerdale, from the north it is possible to use the 77/ 77a bus services and to walk from Gatesgarth (NY 194 149) over Gatesgarth Pass or from the top of Honister Pass (NY 225 135).

   The area can be accessed by the 77c bus service between Cockermouth and Buttermere.

   From the west there is the bus service to Cleator Moor (NY 027 145) but that is quite some way from Ennerdale and the use of a bike should be considered.

Ron Kenyon - 07/10/2023
These fells are rather remote but a plan was hatched to take the bus to the top of Honister Pass and to head for **Kirk Fell**, **Pillar**, **Steeple** *and* **Yewbarrow** *ending up in Wasdale and staying at a climbing hut at Wasdale Head. It seemed a good idea as on the Wednesday before, the weather forecast looked good - however forecasts can change - and it did!*

A welcome sight with the summit trig point on Pillar (Walk **WF7**).

7   KIRK FELL etc - continued

Haskett Buttress, appearing out of the clouds to the west of Steeple (Walk **WF7**).

Heavy cloud hung over the fells but thankfully there was no rain. We took the bus to Keswick then the 77a bus service up Borrowdale. We got talking to a chap from Alberta, Canada, living in Maidstone for a year - he had **Catbells** *in his sights before regaining the bus to go to the Buttermere Youth Hostel where he was staying overnight. Chris disembarked at Seatoller and headed over Sty Head, seeing nothing but a lot of wet mist. I carried on to the top of Honister Pass. Here the cloud was very evident but I got myself ready and headed off upwards. I realised that good navigation and a bit of knowledge of the area would be needed – it would also have been nice to have had a GPS device! Distances seem to lengthen when you are in the mist and it was good to eventually reach Beck Head and the tarns there. I carried on over* **Kirk Fell** *(including North Top - it is a Birkett!) and had a bit of an epic descent to Black Sail Pass. Looking Stead and the path to* **Pillar** *seemed to take ages with subsidiary summits appearing in the mist but eventually I gained its summit. The mist cleared a bit going across to Black Crag and I met a couple of other walkers going in the other direction. Over* **Scoat Fell** *and down to* **Steeple** *I saw some amazing views above the clouds. It was then back over* **Scoat Fell** *and on to* **Red Pike** *(with some more subsidiary summits in the mist). Time was now ticking on and I was pondering about whether there was time for* **Yewbarrow**. *I felt maybe I should drop down from Dore Head but wait and see when I got there. I also realised I did not have a head torch though I had the phone torch. Down and down I went through the mist and odd bits of crag and fell loomed above but eventually I realised I was going along beside* **Yewbarrow** *by Overbeck. It was also getting a bit darker so I continued down, with car lights appearing in the distance, to the road. I could see the lights of folk coming off* **Scafell Pike** *as I plodded along the road and eventually reached the warmth and comfort of the climbing hut. Chris had been following my progress during the day with my texts from various summits but it was good to see her and the folk in the hut and soon settled in around a nice warm fire.*

8 FLEETWITH PIKE

Fleetwith Pike is a fine summit at the head of the Buttermere valley, with its northern slope dropping down to Honister Pass and the ridge leading southwards to link with **Haystacks** and **Grey Knotts**. There is a long ridge leading up from Gatesgarth Farm to its summit as well as a less severe and shorter ascent from the top of Honister Pass.

Honister Slate Mine has made its mark on the north side of Fleetwith Pike.

 The 77 / 77a bus services from Keswick to the Buttermere valley go over Honister Pass and along the Buttermere valley (between March and November) with stops at the top of Honister Pass (NY 225 135) and Gatesgarth Farm (NY 194 194).

 The area can be accessed by the 77c bus service between Cockermouth and Buttermere.

Chris and Ron Kenyon - 27/10/2023
For various reasons nobody had climbed **Fleetwith Pike** *this year without a car - and there was some urgency to get up there with the bus services over Honister Pass stopping on the 5th November.*
Chris and I found ourselves on the 9.15am X4 bus to Keswick then the 77a bus to Honister. The cloud was a little low but not as low as when I was last there with the Kirk Fell trip (Walk **WF7**). *We made our way up to the Drum House then across the fell side and up onto* **Fleetwith Pike**. *The mist and clouds were swirling about and created a great atmosphere. We went up by Black Star and along the ridge there was mist and cloud on the right and sunshine on the left – ideal conditions for a brocken spectre - and as we came to a section with a slight prow there was the spectre off to the right! Views from the summit were superb and we were soon making our way down with a detour to have a look down into the old quarry workings and at the end of the via ferrata. We reached the base and refreshment was called for at the cafe.*
We took the 77a bus through Buttermere and back over Whinlatter to Keswick. We waited for the bus to Penrith but the bus driver said there was no service as there had been a road accident near Troutbeck, on the A66. A chap there had to get to the railway station at Penrith and asked if anyone wanted to share a taxi - which is what we did (it was not a car!) and made our way, without too much bother to Penrith and home.

Memorable moments on Fleetwith Pike - brocken spectre on approach/summit silhouette (Walk **WF8**).

WESTERN FELLS

9 YEWBARROW

Yewbarrow is a bit of a baby in size for the area but has a reputation for a steep ascent, particular for fell runners on the Bob Graham Round, directly up or down from the track leading to the National Trust campsite. It is much better, and more normal, to ascend from the south end, from Overbeck Bridge and/or to link it with **Red Pike** over Stirrup Crag.

   Yewbarrow is near the head of Wasdale to which the Wasdale Shuttle bus travels during the summer months. Overbeck Bridge (NY 168 068) is the normal start point for an ascent.

   There are various routes from surrounding valleys over passes into Wasdale Head.

Jane, Gary and Rona - 22/11/2023
*Following on from the day on the Scafells and Wasdale Screes (Walk **SF5**) we enjoyed a lovely night at the Wasdale Head Inn, but woke to pouring rain and low cloud. We opted for the most direct route (Bob Graham Round) that starts opposite the entrance to the NT car park/campsite, up and down* **Yewbarrow** *before making our way over Sty Head and back to Seatoller. We'd never seen the becks so wild and full as the rain hammered down - all very dramatic. Missing the bus by one minute meant an hour's shiver and some star jumps in the bus shelter. In retrospect, we should have gone for tea and cake in the Glaramara Hotel, just along the road. We were back home by 4.00pm however after a memorable two days on the hill.*

Patience is sometimes needed waiting for the bus - Gary and Rona at the bus shelter at Seatoller (Walk **WF9**) - *photo Jane Meeks.*

162

Looking into Langstrath from Eagle Crag, with Sergeant's Crag and Bowfell behind, en route to Grasmere.

Boarding the bus at Keswick Bus Station.

OTHER SUGGESTED ROUTES

Needless to say there are a huge number and variety of walks and runs which can be taken in the Lake District. The routes detailed in Chapter 7 were those taken by the EVMC members in 2023 - some are popular and logical routes whilst others were adapted to fit what had to be ascended. This chapter gives a few additional ideas.

Valley to Valley

With a vehicle you have to return to the same place. However with public transport this is not necessary and one can start in one valley and finish in another.

A good example of this is with Walk **NW6** using the bus from Keswick to Buttermere and traversing over **Rannerdale Knotts**, **Whiteless Pike**, **Eel Crag** and **Causey Pike** to Newlands Valley before catching the bus back to Keswick.

Another good route from Keswick is to take the bus up Borrowdale, to Stonethwaite, then to ascend **High Raise**, and to descend by one of a number of routes to Grasmere before catching the bus back to Keswick.

At the weekend, in the summer, there is the 509 bus service from Keswick to Patterdale which can be taken to Glenridding in order to ascend **Helvellyn** before descending to Thirlmere or going along the Helvellyn Ridge (Walk **EF5)** before catching the bus to Keswick.

Walk **EF8** is one of a number of interesting links from the Ullswater valley over to Grasmere/Rydal using the Kirkstone Pass bus and then buses on the west side of the Helvellyn Ridge.

George Fisher's Tea Round - this is a 30 mile route with 12,000+ feet of ascent that starts and finishes at the doors of the George Fisher shop in Keswick. This route links together all of the tops that can be viewed out of the top floor café window of the George Fisher shop.

OTHER SUGGESTED ROUTES

Seatree's Day Out - They were fit in those days!

George Seatree was the President of the Fell and Rock Climbing Club in 1910. In the Club Journal of that year, in an article entitled "Reminiscences of Early Lakeland Mountaineers", he recalled an outing that occurred on Good Friday 1874.

The Penrith to Keswick (and Workington) Railway line was opened in 1864 and George lived in Penrith. He and a friend were determined to carry out a reconnoitering expedition and, on the one and only day available, found themselves leaving Penrith by train for Keswick, at 7am, to find out all they could of the terrible Mickledore Chasm - whatever that might be - and the whereabouts and character of the Ennerdale Pillar Stone. Much was crowded into the next memorable twelve hours.

They walked up Borrowdale and followed Grains Gill to Esk Hause and on to **Scafell Pike**. They then dropped down to Mickledore, where they saw Scafell Crag for the first time. (A few years later George climbed the route North or Penrith Climb just to the right of Broad Stand.) They then dropped down to Wasdale Head and went to the Huntsman's Inn (now Wasdale Head Inn), then kept by Auld Will and Dinah Ritson, for lunch. After a hurried meal they bade adieu to the inn and its occupants, crossed Black Sail Pass into Ennerdale, and from Scarth Gap Pass viewed the rugged and steep northern side of the **Pillar** and its Mountain.

Then they continued down to Buttermere and the Fish Inn (now Buttermere Court) for afternoon tea before going over Newlands Pass and back to Keswick to catch the 8.00pm train back to Penrith.

Not a bad day especially when you consider they were probably wearing hobnailed boots.

Multi-Day Trips

Multi-day trips open up loads of possibilities with the ability to stay overnight using hotels, B&Bs, hostels, camping barns, bothies, climbing huts or to camp at an official site or to go wild camping. This needs additional planning, particularly if self-catering or camping, for food and sleeping gear, but this can be hugely satisfying.

The **Bob Graham Round** is a challenge for fell runners to complete in a day however this can make a suitable challenge for walkers when it could be split into a 3 to 5 day trip with a good number of Wainwrights to ascend.

Watersheds

Many of the felltops are on watersheds and walking along these can be very satisfying and allow you to ascend a lot of summits.

There are the classic **Fairfield Horseshoe** (from Ambleside/Rydal) and the **Ennerdale Horseshoe**, both also used for fell races.

OTHER SUGGESTED ROUTES

Here are some more watersheds

Ullswater Valley Watershed

The traverse of the two ridges of the Helvellyn Range and the High Street Ridge makes for a substantial day out. Starting in Threlkeld, with access from the X4/X5 bus, ascend **Clough Head** and follow the ridge over the **Dodds**, **Helvellyn** and **Fairfield** to Kirkstone Pass. Continue onward over **Caudale Moor** to **High Street** then along the ridge over **High Raise**, **Loadpot Hill** and **Arthur's Pike.** There are various ways back to Penrith including the Eamont Way, the bus from Pooley Bridge or over Haughscar Hill, through Askham and along by the River Lowther to Eamont Bridge and Penrith.

Under the Bridge Walk

Footbridge over the River Derwent at Portinscale - start and finish of the *Under the Bridge Walk.*

When starting the Wainwright Relay in 1993 we met someone, just after 6.00am, at the footbridge over the River Derwent at Portinscale, near Keswick. He said he was waiting for some friends to start the Under the Bridge Walk. This follows the watershed of the rivers (Derwent and Greta) which flow under the bridge there and includes **Catbells, Great Gable, Bowfell, Langdale Pikes, High Raise, Helvellyn, Blencathra, Great Calva** and **Skiddaw** - check it out!

OTHER SUGGESTED ROUTES

Cross Lakes Watersheds

On the South to North Watershed - White Pike, above Devoke Water, looking towards Haycock, Pillar, Great Gable, Scafell, Scafell Pike, Esk Pike and Bowfell.

South to North
There is the possibility of a mega-watershed walk from south to north starting at the most southerly summit of Black Combe with the waters of the Rivers Lune and River Eden to the east. This would then go over Yoadcastle, **Harter Fell, Crinkle Crags, Langdale Pikes, Dunmail Raise, Helvellyn, Great Mell Fell, Blencathra, The Knott** and **Longlands Fell** then along to Uldale for a cup of tea to celebrate.

West to East
...and in a West to East direction start at Cleator Moor as with Walk **WF3** and follow the ridge between Ennerdale and Wasdale over **Pillar, Great Gable, Great End** and **Bowfell** to the **Langdale Pikes** and continue over **High Raise** to **Dunmail Raise**. From there head over **Fairfield** to Kirkstone Pass, then go on to **High Street, Harter Fell, Tarn Crag**, Harrop Pike and Yarlside to the A6 at the top of Shap Fell. You would then have to arrange to meet someone there or get your thumb out for a lift!

The 09 Line
If you like going from West to East, this one is most unusual. It is the only West-East grid line which does not cross a lake or tarn taking a straight line walk following the 09 grid line from Wasdale in the west in a direct easterly direction finishing at another Wasdale, by the A6 over Shap Fell, in the east. Navigation is straightforward but it does not cross any summits!

LIST OF WAINWRIGHTS

People have many obsessions for collecting things! For some it started with stamps and train numbers and others with dolls. Many move on to collecting summits with the likes of Munros, Corbetts, Nuttalls and County Tops. It was evident during 2023 that collecting Wainwrights is a very popular pastime for many people. The following is a ticklist for you to use as you ascend the Wainwrights without a car.

For those of you keen on technology there are a number digital summit ticking systems. A popular system is *https://www.hill-bagging.co.uk* - this is the online version of the Database of British and Irish Hills (DoBIH).

Summitbag - *http://summitbag.com* is linked to Strava and ticks off the summits as you reach them.

Looking into Upper Eskdale with Bowfell in the distance.

LIST OF WAINWRIGHTS

No.	FELL	WALK	ALT. (m)	PAGE	DATE	COMPANIONS
1	Scafell Pike	SF5	978	122		
2	Scafell	SF5	964	122		
3	Helvellyn	EF5	950	60		
4	Skiddaw	NF7	931	112		
5	Great End	SF5	910	126		
6	Bowfell	SF4	902	122		
7	Great Gable	WF1	899	150		
8	Pillar	WF7	892	159		
9	Nethermost Pike	EF13	890	68		
10	Catstycam	EF10	889	66		
11	Esk Pike	SF4	885	122		
12	Raise (Helvellyn)	EF5	883	60		
13	Fairfield	EF11	873	66		
14	Blencathra	NF9	868	113		
15	Skiddaw Little Man	NF7	865	112		
16	White Side	EF5	863	60		
17	Crinkle Crags	SF4	858	122		
18	Dollywaggon Pike	EF13	858	68		
19	Great Dodd	EF5	857	60		
20	Grasmoor	NWF9	851	145		
21	Stybarrow Dodd	EF5	844	60		
22	Scoat Fell	WF7	841	159		
23	St. Sunday Crag	EF11	840	66		
24	Eel Crag	NWF6	838	141		
25	High Street	FEF7	828	81		
26	Red Pike (Wasdale)	WF7	828	159		
27	Hart Crag	EF8/11	822	64/66		
28	Steeple	WF7	819	159		
29	Lingmell	SF3	807	121		
30	High Stile	WF4	806	154		
31	Coniston Old Man	SF6	803	128		
32	High Raise (High Street)	FEF9	803	83		
33	Kirk Fell	WF7	802	159		
34	Swirl How	SF6	802	128		
35	Green Gable	WF1	801	150		
36	Haycock	WF3	798	152		
37	Brim Fell	SF6	796	128		
38	Dove Crag	EF8	792	64		
39	Rampsgill Head	FEF9	792	83		
40	Grisedale Pike	NWF9	790	145		
41	Watson's Dodd	EF5	789	60		
42	Great Carrs	SF6	788	128		
43	Allen Crags	SF1	784	118		
44	Glaramara	SF1	783	118		
45	Thornthwaite Crag	FEF6/7	783	79/81		
46	Kidsty Pike	FEF9	780	83		
47	Dow Crag	SF6	779	128		
48	Harter Fell (Mardale)	FEF6	778	79		
49	Red Screes	EF9	776	65		
50	Grey Friar	SF6	773	128		

TICKLIST

No.	FELL	WALK	ALT. (m)	PAGE	DATE	COMPANIONS
51	Sail	NWF6	773	141		
52	Wandope	NWF6	772	141		
53	Hopegill Head	NWF9	770	145		
54	Great Rigg	EF12	766	67		
55	Caudale Moor	FEF7/12	763	81/85		
56	Wetherlam	SF6	763	128		
57	High Raise (*Langstrath*)	CF11	762	99		
58	Slight Side	SF5	762	126		
59	Mardale Ill Bell	FEF6	761	79		
60	Ill Bell	FEF11	757	84		
61	Hart Side	EF14	756	69		
62	Red Pike (*Buttermere*)	WF4	756	154		
63	Dale Head	NWF10	754	146		
64	Carl Side	NF7	746	112		
65	High Crag	WF4	745	154		
66	The Knott	FEF7	739	81		
67	Robinson	NWF10	737	146		
68	Harrison Stickle	CF11	736	99		
69	Seat Sandal	EF13	736	68		
70	Sergeant Man	CF11	736	99		
71	Long Side	NF7	733	112		
72	Kentmere Pike	FEF6	731	79		
73	Hindscarth	NWF10	727	146		
74	Clough Head	EF2/5	726	55/60		
75	Ullscarf	CF8	726	96		
76	Thunacar Knott	CF11	723	99		
77	Froswick	FEF11	719	84		
78	Birkhouse Moor	EF5	718	60		
79	Brandreth	WF1	714	150		
80	Lonscale Fell	NF7	714	112		
81	Branstree	FEF6	713	79		
82	Knott	NF6	710	109		
83	Pike o'Stickle	CF11	708	99		
84	Whiteside	NW9	706	145		
85	Yoke	FEF11	706	84		
86	Pike o'Blisco	SF4	705	122		
87	Bowscale Fell	NF2	703	106		
88	Cold Pike	SF4	701	122		
89	Caw Fell	WF3	697	152		
90	Gray Crag	FEF6	697	79		
91	Pavey Ark	CF11	697	99		
92	Rest Dodd	FEF5	696	78		
93	Grey Knotts	WF1	694	150		
94	Seatallan	WF3	691	152		
95	Great Calva	NF7	690	112		
96	Ullock Pike	NF7	690	112		
97	Bannerdale Crags	NF2	683	106		
98	Loft Crag	CF11	682	99		
99	Sheffield Pike	EF7	675	62		
100	Wether Hill	FEF9	674	83		

170

LIST OF WAINWRIGHTS

No.	FELL	WALK	ALT. (m)	PAGE	DATE	COMPANIONS
101	Bakestall	NF7	673	112		
102	Scar Crags	NWF6	672	141		
103	Loadpot Hill	FEF9	671	83		
104	Tarn Crag (Longsleddale)	FEF6	663	79		
105	Carrock Fell	NF8	661	113		
106	Whiteless Pike	NWF6	660	141		
107	High Pike (Caldbeck)	NF8	657	113		
108	High Pike (Scandale)	EF8	657	64		
109	Place Fell	FEF3	657	76		
110	Selside Pike	FEF6	655	79		
111	Middle Dodd	EF9	654	65		
112	High Spy	NWF8	653	144		
113	Harter Fell (Eskdale)	SF2	652	119		
114	Great Sca Fell	NF6	651	109		
115	Rossett Pike	SF4	651	122		
116	Fleetwith Pike	WF8	648	161		
117	Base Brown	WF1	646	150		
118	Grey Crag	FEF6	638	79		
119	Causey Pike	NWF6	637	141		
120	Little Hart Crag	EF9	637	65		
121	Mungrisdale Common	NF2	633	106		
122	Starling Dodd	WF4	633	154		
123	Seathwaite Fell	SF1	632	118		
124	Yewbarrow	WF9	627	162		
125	Birks	EF11	622	66		
126	Hartsop Dodd	FEF12	618	85		
127	Great Borne	WF4	615	154		
128	Heron Pike	EF12	612	67		
129	High Seat	CF2	608	91		
130	Illgill Head	SF5	608	126		
131	Haystacks	WF2	597	151		
132	Bleaberry Fell	CF4	589	93		
133	Shipman Knotts	FEF6	587	79		
134	Brae Fell	NF6	585	109		
135	Middle Fell	WF3	582	152		
136	Ard Crags	NWF7	581	143		
137	Maiden Moor	NWF8	575	144		
138	The Nab	FEF5	575	78		
139	Blake Fell	WF6	572	156		
140	Sergeant's Crag	CF7	571	95		
141	Hartsop Above How	EF8/11	570	64/66		
142	Outerside	NWF3	568	138		
143	Angletarn Pikes	FEF2	566	75		
144	Brock Crags	FEF2	561	75		
145	Knott Rigg	NWF7	556	143		
146	Blea Rigg	CF12	556	101		
147	Lord's Seat	NWF4	552	139		
148	Steel Fell	CF10	552	99		
149	Rosthwaite Fell (Bessyboot)	SF1	551	118		
150	Hard Knott	SF2	550	119		

TICKLIST

No.	FELL	WALK	ALT. (m)	PAGE	DATE	COMPANIONS
151	Meal Fell	NF6	550	109		
152	Tarn Crag (Easedale)	CF9	549	98		
153	Lank Rigg	WF3	541	152		
154	Calf Crag	CF10	537	99		
155	Great Mell Fell	EF4	536	58		
156	Whin Rigg	SF5	535	126		
157	Arthur's Pike	FEF1/9	532	74/83		
158	Gavel Fell	WF6	526	156		
159	Great Cockup	NF6	526	109		
160	Bonscale Pike	FEF9	524	83		
161	Crag Fell	WF3	523	152		
162	Souther Fell	NF5	522	109		
163	Eagle Crag	CF7	520	95		
164	High Hartsop Dodd	EF9	519	65		
165	Whinlatter	NWF5	517	140		
166	High Tove	CF8	515	96		
167	Sallows	FEF11	515	84		
168	Mellbreak	WF6	512	156		
169	Beda Fell	FEF8	509	82		
170	Broom Fell	NWF4	509	139		
171	Hen Comb	WF6	509	156		
172	Low Pike	EF8	508	64		
173	Little Mell Fell	EF3	505	57		
174	Stone Arthur	EF12	504	67		
175	Dodd	NF3	502	107		
176	Green Crag	SF2	488	119		
177	Grike	WF3	488	152		
178	Wansfell	FEF4	487	77		
179	Longlands Fell	NF6	483	109		
180	Sour Howes	FEF11	483	84		
181	Gowbarrow Fell	EF6	481	61		
182	Armboth Fell	CF8	479	96		
183	Burnbank Fell	WF6	475	156		
184	Lingmoor Fell	SF4	469	122		
185	Barf	NWF4	468	139		
186	Raven Crag	CF5	461	94		
187	Graystones	NWF4	456	139		
188	Barrow	NWF3	455	138		
189	Great Crag	CF3	452	92		
190	Catbells	NWF8	451	144		
191	Binsey	NF4	447	108		
192	Glenridding Dodd	EF1	442	54		
193	Nab Scar	EF12	442	67		
194	Arnison Crag	EF1	434	54		
195	Steel Knotts	FEF10	431	84		
196	Buckbarrow	WF3	430	152		
197	Gibson Knott	CF10	420	99		
198	Fellbarrow	WF5	415	155		
199	Grange Fell	CF3	415	92		
200	Low Fell	WF5	412	155		

LIST OF WAINWRIGHTS

No.	FELL	WALK	ALT. (m)	PAGE	DATE	COMPANIONS
201	Helm Crag	CF10	405	99		
202	Silver How	CF6	394	95		
203	Hallin Fell	FEF8	387	82		
204	Walla Crag	CF4	379	93		
205	Ling Fell	NWF2/4	373	137/139		
206	Latrigg	NF1	367	105		
207	Troutbeck Tongue	FEF11	363	84		
208	Sale Fell	NWF2/4	359	137/139		
209	High Rigg	CF1	357	90		
210	Rannerdale Knotts	NWF6	355	141		
211	Loughrigg Fell	CF6	336	95		
212	Black Crag	SF6	322	128		
213	Holme Fell	SF6	317	128		
214	Castle Crag	NW1	290	136		

Scafell group from Haycock (Walk **WF3**).

BEST VIEWS IN THE LAKE DISTRICT

Views often make a walk, whether from the summit or lower down.
The following is a collection of 12 views in the Lake District which are well worth seeking out - no doubt you will have your own favourites.

What makes a good view? It can often be the conditions with a fine clear day, a wintery day with snow on the fells, a misty cloudy day or looking down onto a cloud inversion.

No less an authority than the Grasmere painter Heaton Cooper, in his book Mountain Painter, indicated that he found "that one gets the best view of a mountain from another opposite and equal to about half the height of the former, being as it were, at right angles to its general slope" – though - "This is not to say that great views of mountains cannot be obtained from the summits or from the lower levels, even from flat valleys or lakes".

Stunning view of Upper Eskdale taken from Border End in December 2014.

1   Arthur's Pike

Just north-west of and slightly lower than the summit of **Arthur's Pike** there is a prominent cairn (NY 459 207) from which there is a fine view over Ullswater and towards the Helvellyn range.

BEST VIEWS

Cairn on Arthur's Pike (NY 459 207) from which there is a fine view over Ullswater towards the Helvellyn range.

2   Ashness Bridge

Ashness Bridge (NY 270 197) is the iconic packhorse bridge, on the road up to Watendlath, and gives a fine vista looking towards Keswick with **Skiddaw** behind. There are fine views, looking out over Derwentwater, from the car parks just above Ashness Bridge and about ½ mile further on - one of these is known as Surprise View - the other is also a surprise!

3   Border End

Border End (NY 228 018) is the west subsidiary summit of **Hard Knott**, above the pass of the same name. It has a fine vista up Upper Eskdale looking towards the **Scafells**, to the left, and round to **Bowfell** and **Crinkle Crags**. The painter Heaton Cooper commented on the view from **Hard Knott** in his book Mountain Painter, comparing it to the view of the Matterhorn from the Gornergrat and the Chamonix Aiguilles from the Aiguilles Rouge. More of the paintings of the Heaton Cooper family can be seen at their studio in Gramere.   www.heatoncooper.co.uk

4   Castle Head

Castle Head (NY 270 226) is right next to the Borrowdale road, on the outskirts of Keswick, and is well worth ascending in its own right for what must be one of the best views in the Lakes for the least effort. It was used by the film director Ken Russell in his 1975 film Tommy with Roger Daltry (of the group The Who) playing the Pinball Wizard. There was a scene of him (it was actually the local climber Ray McHaffie) running up **Haystacks**, with Buttermere behind, but then topping out on Castle Head. If you didn't know the area you would not notice the difference. I am sure Roger Daltry enjoyed the view like everyone else!

Local artist Benni Fish in action painting the view from the summit of Castle Head.
Benni lives near Cockermouth and his paintings can be seen on the website
https://bojfish.wixsite.com/benjaminfish
and Instagram @bennifish.art

5 Green Hill (Gowbarrow Fell)

Green Hill (NY 409 210) is the southern subsidiary summit of **Gowbarrow Fell** from where there is a fine view of the upper reaches of Ullswater with **St Sunday Crag** and **Fairfield** beyond.

6 Lingmoor

The Langdale Pikes form such a prominent skyline and can be seen from many locations, such as Orrest Head, Loughrigg Tarn, **Wansfell** and even the M6. It is difficult to say which is the best but that from near the summit of **Lingmoor** (NY 300 048), with some cloud in the valley, is quite something.

A magical time in February 2015 when walking from the summit of Lingmoor to Side Pike with clouds in the valley and Bowfell and Langdale Pikes beyond.

BEST VIEWS

7 Lowthwaite Fell (Low Fell)

Lowthwaite Fell (NY 136 223) is the subsidiary summit of Low Fell, above Kirkstile, and gives a great view up the Buttermere valley as well as across to the fells to the south of Loweswater.

8 Orrest Head

Very close to the Windermere railway station, Orrest Head (SD 414 993) can be ascended quickly and is highly recommended if you have a few hours to spare before catching a train or a bus. In 1930 this was to give Alfred Wainwright his first view of the Lakeland fells and his inspiration. It is not a "Wainwright" but this is where it all started!

"Those few hours on Orrest Head cast a spell which changed my life!" AW

9 Skiddaw Little Man

Skiddaw towers over Keswick and gives a fine backdrop to the town when looking down Borrowdale. Looking the other way the view from the summit of **Skiddaw** is rather disappointing, however the nearby summit of **Skiddaw Little Man** (NY 266 278) is a different matter with its steep slopes dropping away to give a fine vista over Keswick to Borrowdale and beyond.

10   Symonds Knott

When on the summit of **Scafell**, it is well worth making a slight diversion to the summit of Symonds Knott (NY 207 067). This is just north of the main summit and is a subsidiary summit (and over 3,000 feet and third highest point in the Lake District) between the path dropping down the west ridge to Wasdale and Deep Gill, which is the gully splitting the crag. From its summit there is an extensive view over to **Pillar**, **Great Gable** and beyond as well as the rock pinnacle of Scafell Pinnacle in the foreground.

11   Wasdale

If you don't fancy walking anywhere for your view this is the one for you. Near the bottom end of Wastwater, just east of the road junction and near the lake, there is "THAT VIEW" (NY 152 054).

The head of the valley is encircled by **Yewbarrow, Great Gable, Scafell Pike** and **Scafell** together with the Wasdale Screes dropping into the lake on the right.

12   Westmorland Cairn

When on **Great Gable** it is well worth going to Westmorland Cairn (NY 210 102), which is just south-west of the main summit and above Westmorland Crag. Here there is the stunning view over Wasdale, with Great Hell Gate dropping away below, and **Lingmell** and **Scafell Pike** across the valley. The cairn was originally built by the grandfather of Rusty Westmorland - Rusty was the founder of the Borrowdale Rescue Team which became the Keswick MRT.

Above: View 5 over the upper reaches of Ullswater from Green Hill, the southern subsidiary summit of Gowbarrow Fell.

BEST VIEWS

Above: The summit area of Great Gable suddenly drops away over Westmorland Crag to give this stunning view from Westmorland Cairn.

WAINWRIGHT ROUNDS AND RELAYS

For most, the completion of all the Wainwrights will take many years - for some it will take a little less time!

Wainwright Rounds

In 1981, Chris Bland, cousin of fell runner Billy Bland, decided to inaugurate the Wainwrights Challenge as a means to raise money for repairs to his local church in Borrowdale valley, for which he was a warden. Sited on the outskirts of the hamlet of Stonethwaite, it is the church where Bob Graham lies buried. Chris's plan was to climb the summits in each of the pictorial guides over consecutive days, thus completing seven books in seven days. To this he added a further constraint with each day starting and finishing at a valley church, reflecting his cause.

The first recorded continuous Wainwright Round was that by Alan Heaton in 1985 in 9 days and 16 hours - a tremendous achievement by a veteran of many ultra challenges.

In 1987, another fell running legend - Joss Naylor - made a complete traverse of the Wainwrights in an amazing 7 days, 1 hour and 25 minutes. This followed a route put together with his pal Ken Ledward which weaved around the Lake District covering the 214 summits in the most efficient way that they could devise. Details are available in the booklet "Joss Naylor MBE was Here".

Joss's record for the Wainwrights, like many of his records, remained for many years until Steve Birkenshaw set his sights on it. An exceptional orienteer and fell runner, Steve looked at the route taken by Joss and fine-tuned it with new eyes to produce a route covering a distance of about 320 miles and 118,000 feet of ascent. In 2014 he was at the Moot Hall ready with his team and 6 days, 12 hours and 58 minutes later he returned there after a dramatic run which he recalled in his appropriately named book "There is No Map in Hell".

Others followed in his steps with the time taken being reduced by Paul Tierney in 2019 and then Sabina Verjee in 2021 - an account of which is recorded in her book "Where There's a Hill" - when she reduced the time to just under 6 days.

Between 2 – 7 May 2022 the American John Kelly took up the challenge and knocked 11.5 hours off Sabrina's time to complete the Wainwrights in 5 days, 12 hours and 14 minutes.

In December 2021 James Gibson completed the first winter traverse of the Wainwrights in an astonishing, and no doubt chilly, 8 days, 6 hours and 43 minutes.

Over the new year between December 2024 and January 2025, in somewhat harsh conditions, Carol Morgan reduced this time and completed a winter traverse in 8 days, 1 hour, 51 minutes.

Who will step up next to lower the times?

Wainwright Relay

In 1993, Harry Blenkinsop, a member of the Eden Valley MC, came up with the idea of following Joss's route as a relay. We had a team of four pairs and divided the route up into reasonably manageable sections with one section per pair, per day, over roughly a four day schedule.
The team was made up of Jon Bardgett, Gary Baum, Phil Blanshard, Harry Blenkinsop, Al Davis, Ron Kenyon, Jane Meeks and Pete Teasdale.
The Moot Hall, in Keswick, is the traditional starting point for such challenges and at 6.00am the first pair set off. There were many memorable moments which followed such as:

- The shock to the system of a mega-long first leg encircling Bassenthwaite.
- Turning right and dropping off Yoke down the "vertical" slope to Troutbeck Tongue.
- Entering a foggy Armboth bog and emerging completely exhausted and covered in black ooze a few hours later.
- Running under the full moon over Fellbarrow and Low Fell and missing a pint at the Kirkstile Inn.

We eventually finished back at the Moot Hall 4 ½ days later. We felt the celebratory drink was well deserved, but our achievement gave us a small insight into the ability and tenacity of the likes of Joss Naylor who kept going, day in and day out, for over a week.

In 2021, Durham Fell Runners took up the challenge of a Wainwright Relay, following Steve Birkenshaw's route, and successfully completed the relay, with 27 runners and 2 dogs, in a time of 4 days, 6 hours, 50 minutes and 15 seconds - details are on their website: www.durhamfellrunners.org

There is something special about running as a relay team. Running the full Wainwright Round is unimaginable for most runners but running in a relay team is much more feasible. Also now with mobile phones, Strava and following "that dot", communication and the management of long runs is somewhat easier.

Any clubs, out there, up for the challenge to break 4 days?

GLOSSARY

This is a Glossary giving details about various places in and aspects of the Lake District mentioned in this book and I hope it helps to inform you about the area and what there is here.

Alan Roper	183
Armitt Museum	183
Birketts	184
The Bishop	184
The Bob Graham Round	184
Climbing Huts	185
Coniston Coppermines	185
Fred Whitton Cycle Challenge	185
The Great Gift	185
Greenside Mines	186
Halifax Bomber crash on Great Carrs	186
Honister Slate Mine	187
Keswick Museum and Art Gallery	187
Mountain Heritage Trust	187
John Ruskin and Brantwood	188
Ruskin Museum	188
Skiing and Ski-touring	189
Steve Parr Round	189
Threlkeld Quarry	189
The Wainwright Society	190
William Wordsworth and Grasmere	191

Left: EVMC Wainwright Relay Team - copyright with Cumberland and Westmorland Herald.

GLOSSARY OF TERMS AND LOCATIONS

Alan Roper (route **NWF6**)

Alan has drawn and painted most of his life, although it was not until the age of 13 that he cycled up into the Lakes, from his home at Aspatria, with a sketch pad and pencils.

His current work as a graphic artist and designer includes painting landscapes and maps as viewed from the air, turning reference material into aerial views using imagination. This has been helped by an understanding of how shapes and their shadows look in perspective, knowledge gained by painting out of doors. After training at an art college, he has found that creating artwork outside, after a walk up a fell side or a cycle ride to a lake, brings a sense of urgency to the work as there is usually a race against the weather.

This results in a look of spontaneity and emphasis - clean, exciting lines for the drawing and decisive brushwork. It can also result in economy of mark making - one mark in the right place can equal ten in the wrong place. Working outdoors in a wind really sharpens the mind, and allows you to really see the three dimensional shapes and their shadows that make up the subject and record these more convincingly on paper.

Armitt Museum

This is a museum in Ambleside where there are interesting displays about Ambleside and the wider Lakeland area. In 2023 there were the following displays:

✳ The Armitt explores - The Armitt sisters, in particular Mary Louisa Armitt, who had the original idea of a museum in Ambleside.

✳ Learning through the Natural World - Charlotte Mason established her House of Education in Ambleside in 1892. The school was a learning institution for governesses where students learnt to teach the home-educated children of the professional middle classes of the late Victorian era. This developed over time and became the Charlotte Mason College.

It is now the University of Cumbria, Ambleside campus.

✳ Beatrix Potter; Passions in Paint - Beatrix Potter had close links with the area and left over 300 fine drawings of fungi to the museum.

Quite a collection of inspirational ladies!

In 2024 there was a major display about fell running entitled "Running int' Fells".

In 2025 there is an exhibition about Alfred Wainwright - "Discover the man behind the 214 fells".

It is well worth popping in to see what is on display to learn about the area.

More information on - *www.armitt.com*

Birketts

These are the 541 English peaks described in Bill Birkett's book, Complete Lakeland Fells. The author defined them as all the fells within the boundary of the Lake District National Park in Cumbria which are over 1,000 feet (304.8 m) in height.

Bill's book has become a popular list for peak-bagging in the Lake District, along with the Wainwrights. Because both lists are based on historical books, unlike for example the Munros, their constituents remain fixed, regardless of revisions to height or other metrics. In this regard, The Long Distance Walkers Association maintains a register of people who have completed the Birketts.

The Bishop

Barf is an outlier of Lord's Seat in the Whinlatter Forest area. On the side of Barf, overlooking Thornthwaite, is a distinctive rock which is called "The Bishop". This marks the spot where, according to local legend, the Bishop of Derry was killed falling from his horse in 1783, after drunkenly betting he could ride up the hill. The bishop was laid to rest at the base of the mountain and to commemorate his rather foolhardy enterprise the rock, known as the Bishop's Clerk, was painted white by patrons of the Swan, who have since then maintained "The Bishop" in his pristine white coat. The fee paid to patrons painting the rock was set at one shilling and a quart of ale. Since the hotel closed, local villagers have continued this tradition.

The Bob Graham Round

The Bob Graham Round (BG) is a challenge, established by Bob Graham, in 1932, with the ascent of 42 summits, around the Lake District, in 24 hours. He was 42 years old at the time hence the number of summits. This is regularly attempted, especially during the summer, by accomplished ultra-distance runners - you will likely see a throng gathered near the top of Dunmail Raise at the time of the full moon.

There is a total distance of about 66 miles and 27,000 feet of ascent.

Further details on *http://bobgrahamclub.org.uk*

Jeevendra Singh, the first Indian to complete the BG, on 25/09/2024.

Climbing Huts

There are a number of properties (Climbing Huts) around the Lake District owned by various climbing clubs. These huts are private and available for use only by club members or, if the club is affiliated to the British Mountaineering Council (BMC), then the hut may be available to members of the BMC.

Coniston Coppermines

Mining for copper in the valley above Coniston dates back to the 16th century and the area continued to be mined until the 1950s. Industrial mining of copper at Coniston is said to have started in the 1690s after Elizabeth I brought over German miners to exploit the local deposits at Keswick in the mid 1500s. In 1859 the Coniston Railway was opened, between Broughton and Coniston, to transport the copper ore – this was closed on the 30th April 1962.

Today there are industrial remains of the industry and the Coniston Coppermines Youth Hostel is based in the old manager's building.

More details are available on *www.catmhs.org.uk*.

Fred Whitton Cycle Challenge

This is a cycling challenge around the Lake District over six passes - Kirkstone Pass, Honister Pass, Newlands Pass, Whinlatter Pass, Hard Knott Pass and Wrynose Pass.

It can be done individually or as part of the annual organised event, usually held in May.

More details are available on
www.fredwhittonchallenge.co.uk

The Great Gift

The Fell and Rock Climbing Club (FRCC) is one of the main climbing clubs in the United Kingdom and was established in 1906. Sadly, during WWI, 21 members of the Club were killed and the Club wanted to acquire a memorial to these members. The Club eventually purchased land at the heads of Wasdale and Borrowdale, at over 1,500 feet, which contained the following 12 summits - Kirk Fell, Great Gable, Green Gable, Brandreth, Grey Knotts, Base Brown, Glaramara, Allen Crags, Seathwaite Fell, Great End, Broad Crag and Lingmell. In 1924, the FRCC gave all this land to the National Trust and the nation and this was known as The Great Gift. There is a memorial plaque on the summit of Great Gable and a remembrance service is held on Great Gable on Remembrance Sunday, each year, which is open for anyone to attend.

Greenside Lead Mine, near Glenridding

The Greenside Lead Mine was a successful lead mine between 1825 and 1961. It produced approximately 250,000 tons of lead and 1,600,000 ounces (45 tons) of silver, from around 3 million tons of ore. During the 1940s it was the only large-scale producer of lead ore in the UK.

The earliest known date the mine opened was the mid 1750s but it had closed by the early 1800s. In 1825 the Greenside Mining Company was formed and reopened the mine. Mining activities traced the Greenside Vein, a mineral vein which filled a geological fault running in a north–south direction through the east ridge of Green Side, between Stybarrow Dodd and Hart Side. This fault had a length of 3,900 feet (1,200m) and went to a depth of 2,900 feet (880m) - the lowest point in the mine being 322 feet (100m) below sea level. Electricity was introduced to the mine in the 1890s and it became the first metalliferous mine in the UK to use electric winding engines and an electric locomotive. Electricity was generated by hydro-power using water from the natural Keppelcove Tarn. After exceptionally heavy rain the front of the tarn collapsed on 28th/29th October 1927 and much flood damage was caused in Glenridding. A dam was then built but this burst in August 1931.

The mine closed in 1962 after lead reserves had been exhausted. Just before it closed the mine was used by the Atomic Weapons Research Establishment (AWRE) to conduct an experiment detecting seismic signals from underground explosions.

Fifteen years after the mine closed mine explorers began to visit the upper levels. Between 1992 and 1996 they reopened the main level and cleared several roof falls, and today they are able to pass through the mine using an old escape route.

Halifax Bomber crash on Great Carrs

On 22nd October 1944 there was a tragic aircraft accident on the Coniston fells. It was a typical autumn night with the southern fells covered in thick dark cloud. The roar of the four Rolls-Royce Merlin engines fitted to the Halifax bomber LL505-S was heard flying over the Three Shires Inn in Little Langdale, on a night flying exercise. Sadly, seconds later, the sixteen ton bomber hit Top Broad Slack between the summits of Swirl How and Great Carrs, exploding immediately and bursting into flames.

A memorial was later erected at the site of the accident in the form of an engraved stone topped by a cross. Sadly, over the years there have been many aircraft accidents on the Lake District fells.

Honister Slate Mine
This is the last working slate mine in England. Quarrying for Westmorland green slate has been taking place in the area since 1643. As capacity has increased, the site's underground workings have been extensively expanded.

By 1870 underground workings at the mine stretched under Honister Crag with intermediate workings on the opposite side of the valley at Yew Crags as well as smaller-scale underground workings on Dubbs Moor, together with a small opencast quarry.

By 1891 production had reached 3,000 tons a year and more than 100 men were employed in the mines.

There have been various owners over the years working the mines. In 1997 the mine was reopened by local businessman, Mark Weir, who redeveloped the mining side, producing small quantities of roofing slate, also turning the site into a tourist attraction. Sadly, Mark died in 2011 but his family continue to run the mine as well as the connected via-ferrata, zip wire and mine tours.

Keswick Museum and Art Gallery
This was founded in 1873 by the Keswick Literary and Scientific Society and moved into the present premises, in Fitz Park, in 1898. This was the earliest purpose-built museum in Cumbria. Only a small selection of the 20,000 items in the museum collection are on display at any one time, but these give a fine insight into the Keswick area.

There is a large exhibition room with displays which change on a regular basis.
More information on - https://keswickmuseum.org.uk

Mountain Heritage Trust
This is an organisation set up by the mountain-loving community to preserve and celebrate mountain heritage. There is a dedicated team committed to safeguarding the stories, traditions, and legacies woven into the rugged mountain landscapes of the Lake District and beyond. The Trust is based at the Blencathra Centre, above Threlkeld, and more details are available on the website - *www.mountain-heritage.org*

John Ruskin and Brantwood

Brantwood is a fine building on the east side of Coniston Water. It was the residence of John Ruskin (1819 – 1900) who was an English writer, philosopher, art historian, art critic and polymath of the Victorian era. He wrote on subjects as varied as geology, architecture, myth, ornithology, literature, education, botany and political economy.

Ruskin authored several works on political economy and his social view broadened from concerns about the dignity of labour to consider issues of citizenship and notions of the ideal community. He was hugely influential in the latter half of the 19th century and up to the First World War. After a period of relative decline, his reputation has steadily improved since the 1960s with the publication of numerous academic studies of his work. Today, his ideas and concerns are widely recognised as having anticipated interest in environmentalism, sustainability and craft.

In 1878, he set up the philanthropic "Guild of St George". This represented Ruskin's practical response to a society in which profit and mass-production seemed to be everything and beauty, goodness and ordinary happiness nothing.

He was a great thinker and influenced many people during and after his life including John Muir, the father of the National Parks in the United States.

In the Lake District he was involved with opposition to the extension of the railway to Ambleside and also against the creation of the Thirlmere Reservoir by Manchester Corporation. In various ways these were partly instrumental in the formation of the National Trust by Canon Hardwicke Rawnsley, Robert Hunter and Octavia Hill in 1895.

Brantwood was his home for many years and a meeting place of many like-minded great names of that time - and is still a fantastic place to visit and contemplate the world. Details of John Ruskin and Brantwood are available on the website - htpps://www.brantwood.org.uk

Ruskin Museum

This is set in the heart of Coniston Village and tells the fascinating 'Story of Coniston' including details of the many people who have lived and worked here.

 The museum is named after John Ruskin, the Victorian polymath, who lived at Brantwood, on the east side of Coniston Water.

 More recently Donald Campbell was, sadly, killed on Coniston Water in 1967, attempting to break the World Water Speed Record and the museum records his life.

More details available on - *https://ruskinmuseum.com*

Skiing and Ski-touring

The Lake District is NOT a skiing mecca. However, with the right conditions, it is well worth getting the skiing gear into action.
There is a permanent ski-lift located on Raise, near Helvellyn; this is owned and run by the Lake District Ski Club - *https://www.ldscsnowski.co.uk*
This ski-lift was first established in the 1950s by local enthusiasts with the engine for the towing system taken up using a land rover by Frank Keiser, aided and abetted by his pals George Rigg and Jack Savage. There have been many improvements over the years. The system is run entirely by volunteers and it is well worth the two mile walk up the fell side when conditions are suitable.
Ski-touring is a style of skiing, without using ski-lifts to ascend, using special skis with skins (used to be seal skins) which are attached to the base of the ski. These are used to ascend slopes and at the summit the skins are detached and you then ski down.
Lake District ski conditions can be somewhat fickle but if the conditions are "IN" then, if possible, go out and ski that day - the next day could be too late!

Steve Parr Round

This is a challenge, linking together all the fells in Lake District over 2500 feet, which dates back to the 1960s when run by Steve Parr. It covers 66 peaks and 116 miles - in 2023 the record was about 33 hours! Sadly, Steve went missing while exploring in the Karakoram area but the legacy of his round is still there.

Threlkeld Quarry

The Threlkeld Quarry & Mining Museum is situated on the side of Clough Head to the south of Threlkeld. The quarry and museum have been lovingly run by knowledgeable and dedicated staff for over 25 years and the site and collections continue to expand.
The museum offers activities for all, from budding geologists to hopeful prospectors, including -
- A narrow gauge railway that runs into the old quarry
- A comprehensive geological and mining museum
- The quarry site with a unique collection of machinery
- Mineral panning

More details on the *https://www.threlkeldquarryandminingmuseum.co.uk*

The Wainwright Society

The inaugural meeting of The Wainwright Society was held on 9th November 2002 at Ambleside Youth Hostel. This was followed by a walk to the summit of Dove Crag, the walk described on the first page of The Eastern Fells penned by AW fifty years earlier.

Our primary aims are to keep alive the fell walking traditions promoted by Alfred Wainwright through his guidebooks and other publications and to keep faith with his vision of introducing a wider audience to fell walking and caring for the hills.

The aims of the Society are articulated through our Objects, which underpin all the Society's activities. These have included: the purchase of the Wainwright Notebook; annotated maps, sketches and other written material, which have been donated to the Cumbria Archive Centre in Kendal; the replacement of the View Indicator and a contribution to new summit seating on Orrest Head; and the re-publication of four out-of-print books written by Wainwright: A Pennine Journey, The Outlying Fells of Lakeland, Walks in Limestone Country and Walks on the Howgill Fells.

The Society has, over the years, raised close to £200,000 for causes which we believe Wainwright would have appreciated and supported. In 2023 we raised £12,750 for Mountain Rescue Cumbria. In 2024, over £17,000 was raised for Fix the Fells, including matched funding from the Lake District Foundation. Our main income source is our annual calendar which is sold mainly through our website.

We welcome new members and you can find out more and join the Society here: *https://www.wainwright.org.uk/membership*

555 bus service passing through Wordsworth Country in Grasmere - *photo Stagecoach.*

William Wordsworth and Grasmere Area

William Wordsworth was born in Cockermouth in 1770. Sadly he was only eight when his mother died and, a year later, he was sent away to school at the Hawkshead Grammar School.
Here he received an exceptional education under the headmaster, William Taylor, with a fine grounding in maths and classics which led to him going to Cambridge University in 1787. He was dissatisfied with the course

Painting of the road outside Dove Cottage by TM Richardson - 1784 - 1828 (*Wordsworth Trust*).

and took greater pleasure in a walking tour, in 1790, of France, the Alps and Italy. He returned to France for a year at the end of 1791, where he fell in love with Annette Vallon, who bore him a daughter. This was the time of the French Revolution and Wordsworth was forced to return to London. With the stability and inspiration of his sister Dorothy and friendships with the likes of Samuel Taylor-Coleridge life moved forward.

In 1799 William Wordsworth arrived in Grasmere aged 29, largely unknown and writing innovative poetry in a new style. In 1802 he married Mary Hutchinson and whilst living at Dove Cottage with his family, Wordsworth wrote many of his greatest poems and his sister Dorothy kept her Grasmere journal.

Dove Cottage did not provide enough space for the Wordsworths' growing family and many visitors, and they left Dove Cottage for Allan Bank, above Grasmere, in May 1808. William had condemned this house as an eyesore when it was first built! Allan Bank was later acquired by Canon Hardwicke Rawnsley, one of the founders of the National Trust, and was left by him to the National Trust and is now open to the public. The Wordsworths moved on again, in 1810, to the Old Rectory in the centre of Grasmere. Rydal Mount, lies between Ambleside and Grasmere and commands glorious views of Windermere, Rydal Water and the surrounding fells. This was Wordsworths' best-loved family home for the greater part of his life, from 1813, to his death in 1850 at the age of 80.

In 1843 he had succeeded Robert Southey as Poet Laureate. Many of the literary and intellectual giants of the time would have visited the Wordsworths - wouldn't it be great to have been a fly on the wall at Dove Cottage or Rydal Mount?

The Wordsworth Trust (*www.wordsworth.org.uk*) brings art and literature alive for tens of thousands of people every year. As well as Dove Cottage, other historic buildings and the new museum it looks after a unique collection of works by Wordsworth and the other writers and artists of the Romantic period. At the heart of this collection are the manuscripts that Wordsworth's descendants gave to the Wordsworth Trust in 1935 so that they could remain here, where they were largely written.

FIX THE FELLS   www.fixthefells.co.uk

Fix the Fells is a partnership between the National Trust, the Lake District National Park Authority, Natural England, the Lake District Foundation and Friends of the Lake District. Its mission is to protect the spectacular Lakeland fells from erosion by repairing and maintaining upland paths and their immediate surroundings, so as to enhance nature and the experience of those in the fells.

The practical work of Fix the Fells is carried out by rangers and volunteers. Four teams of National Trust rangers, who are highly skilled upland path crafts people, use a mix of traditional and innovative techniques to halt and repair upland erosion, manage water flow across routes, protect habitats around paths and create a sustainable line for path users. The practical work is also supported by the Lake District National Park Authority with a dedicated ranger and through the volunteer scheme. A large and dedicated group of volunteers regularly walk all the upland paths year-round to keep on top of basic maintenance, help build and repair them on work parties and support Fix the Fells in many other ways.

The Lake District National Park has never been more popular. Today, residents, along with 18 million visitors a year enjoy walks in the fells. Historically, this resulted in extensive erosion scars, some over 35m wide and 4m deep, which blighted the landscape in the 1990s. An example of one of these scars can be seen in this photograph taken in 1998 of the path up Redacre Gill, on Pike o'Blisco, in Great Langdale. The mountainous landscape, with its combination of both peaty and thin soils, plus steep gradients, is particularly vulnerable to the volume of people in the fells, and to the impacts of climate change. In addition, the frequency and severity of rainfall events is increasing with the climate crisis, further accelerating erosion.

The scar on the Redacre Gill path, on Pike o'Blisco in 1998.

Feet, hoofs and mountain bikes wear away vegetation over time, leaving exposed soils which release carbon into the air and reduce water retention capacity. Heavy rain then washes away the soils, which end up in lakes, where they can be harmful to aquatic life. Habitat alongside paths is damaged, with knock-on impacts on fell plants, insects and animals. Erosion scars become ugly and routes challenging and unappealing to use. With the pressing twin crises today in climate and nature, and the enduring appeal of the fells for days out, the work of Fix the Fells has never been needed more. In the late 1970s, The National Trust, the Lake District National Park Authority and English Nature (now part of Natural England) started working together to try to tackle the issue of erosion. In 1993, they formed the Lake District Upland Access Management Group to find funding for the path work and to coordinate the work of the National Trust and Lake District National Park Authority ranger teams.

FIX THE FELLS

In 2000, a successful bid was made for Heritage Lottery funding and in 2001 Fix the Fells was formed as the vehicle for this funding. The first tranche of Heritage Lottery funding was for a £2.5 million project which ran for 5 years to 2006. A further £2.9m was won in 2005 to cover work up to 2011.

Work on the path from Kirkstone Pass to Caudale Moor by Fix the Fells in September 2024.

This second tranche of Heritage Lottery funding envisaged the setting up of a volunteer scheme, primarily aimed at protecting the legacy of the capital investment by starting a programme of regular path maintenance. In 2007, the Fix the Fells volunteer scheme was started and there are now over 150 registered volunteers. Volunteers come from all walks of life but they are all passionate about giving something back to the landscape they love. A full-time National Trust Volunteer Development Ranger is employed by Fix the Fells to provide help and support to the volunteers. The volunteer scheme is so successful that it is greatly over-subscribed each year when the recruitment window opens each January.
In 2023, volunteers contributed 2,768 volunteer days to Fix the Fells. 1,598 days (just over half) were spent maintaining the paths (removing loose stone, clearing drains etc). The rest of the days were spent doing minor path repairs, under the supervision of either a National Trust ranger or one of the more experienced volunteers.
In 2015, following Storm Desmond, an application for funding was submitted by the Lake District National Park Authority to the Flood Recovery Project, funded by the Rural Payments Agency. A grant of £850,000 was awarded to fund work in 2017 and 2018, which allowed much of the major damage caused by Storm Desmond to be repaired. Between 2011 and 2017, Fix the Fells was funded by support from its partners and generous donations from local businesses, organisations with an interest in the environment and the public.

FIX THE FELLS

In 2018 Fix the Fells successfully applied for £1.5m of funding from the European Regional Development Fund, which funded work carried out between 2019 and 2023. During this period over 29km of paths were repaired.

Fix the Fells remains a partnership of the National Trust, Lake District National Park Authority, Natural England, Friends of the Lake District and the Lake District Foundation. Minimising the impact of path work on the landscape is of major importance, so work will only be carried out on the fell if there is damage that needs repairing. Traditional and innovative new techniques are blended to create resilient surfaces which are better able to withstand the increasing number of visitors and severe weather events. Fix the Fells repairs damage to the fells in a sustainable and considered way.

Work is prioritised mainly by assessing the current and potential visual impact of the erosion on the landscape, the current and potential impact of the erosion on heritage (including ecology, archaeology, geology and other heritage interests) and rate of change in the condition of the path. Other considerations include how easy it is for people to use the path, the availability of funding and the popularity of the route.

Sixteen National Trust rangers work full time for Fix the Fells between April and October to work on the major, and/or technically complex, path projects. Where necessary, stone from nearby fells is sensitively gathered into one tonne bags and flown to the work sites by helicopter. These heli-lifts are planned to avoid any impact on bird nesting sites. The work is physically very hard, taking place high on the fells, in often harsh weather conditions, in remote locations, on rough terrain, and in areas of environmental sensitivity.

Various techniques are used to protect paths from further erosion. Stone pitching is used on the steeper sections. This ancient technique involves digging stone into the ground to form good solid footfalls. The resulting surface is hard-wearing and low maintenance and blends well into the surroundings. However, it can be uncomfortable to walk on, particularly in descent, and is very time-consuming to install.

FIX THE FELLS

Sub-soiling or soil inversion is generally used where the gradient of the path is below 15°. This can be done by hand but often a mechanical digger will construct a turfed ditch. The sub-soil material removed from the ditch is placed alongside to produce a solid, hard-wearing walking surface. A specialised grass seed mix is then sown to encourage a rapid re-generation of the vegetation to bind all the works together. Within a couple of growing seasons the repaired route can look as though there has never been any damage.

Some of the work is designed to make the existing path more attractive to walk on by pitching up to big steps, that people would otherwise choose to walk around, or by installing drains to keep the path surface drier. Once the path has been improved, landscaping is done on any side paths to repair the damage to ensure the path blends in with the surroundings.

The Redacre Gill path (pictured left) was pitched in 2004 to provide a single, sustainable line for walkers. As people no longer spread out, the vegetation on the scar recovers and a long drain was constructed to take water off the path and into the gully to avoid erosion by water.

Redacre Gill path 2021.

Fix the Fells team working on Sticks Path above Great Langdale in April 2023.

FIX THE FELLS

Looking towards High Seat - 2018 vs 2022 - work done in 2021.

This path forms part of a route along the tops of the fells between Derwentwater/Borrowdale and Thirlmere which includes four Wainwrights and is therefore popular with "fell baggers". It is a designated Site of Special Scientific Interest and, along with the other Lake District High Fells, supports a huge area of blanket bog. Upland peat bogs act like sponges, storing water and slowing the flow of water into our rivers. This provides both flood relief during heavy rainfall as water soaks into the peat instead of rushing into the rivers, as well as easing the pressure in droughts as water drains gradually from peat into rivers to keep them flowing. Healthy peat also captures and stores carbon, helping mitigate against the effects of climate change.

The flattish, lowest section of the path between High Tove and High Seat is called the Pewits and it had become unsafe to cross due to years of unabated erosion. There was no safe or dry route through this section, so walkers and livestock were forced ever wider searching for a dry route, spreading the erosion further. These recreational and grazing pressures had damaged the peat which had dried out and eroded. In its degraded state, water runs off the surface of the bog, rather than being absorbed into it. This run-off also carries a lot of dissolved organic carbon into the catchments of rivers and drinking water supplies, causing problems for native wildlife and increasing the treatment costs of drinking water.

In another example of organisations coming together to protect the landscape, a partnership between the National Trust's Riverlands project, Cumbria Wildlife Trust, United Utilities, Fix the Fells and Natural England was formed to restore the peat bog and reverse the damage.
The work aimed to restore the blanket bog in, and to provide a dry sustainable path through, the Pewits. Dry and hagged exposed peat surfaces were re-profiled, bunded and seeded with sphagnum and other species to restore a vibrant wetland habitat.
Various options were considered for the path including subsoiling and board walks. In the end, a combination of stone flags and stretches of subsoiling were settled upon. Stone flags have been used extensively in the Peak District and other places but this is the first upland flagged path in the Lake District.

FIX THE FELLS

The Lake District is under pressure like never before from the growing number of visitors and more extreme weather. Over 18 million people a year visit the National Park, experiencing the physical, mental health and well-being benefits of such beautiful surroundings. But this creates challenges for the mountain environment, with boots, bikes and heavy rain creating unsightly erosion scars and damaging the fragile biodiversity. The work of Fix the Fells is more important than ever, maintaining 408km of upland paths and monitoring known erosion problems on a further 388km of paths.

In the 23 years since it was formed, over £11m has been invested by Fix the Fells in repairing upland paths across the Lake District National Park. Fix the Fells is entirely reliant upon donations to deliver its vital work going.

Further examples of its projects, together with details of how to donate, can be found on its website *www.fixthefells.co.uk*

Team working on the path up Mousthwaite Comb on Blencathra in October 2023.

EDEN VALLEY MOUNTAINEERING CLUB

EVMC Group - Moonlit walk at end of Striding Edge - *photo Gary Baum.*

The Eden Valley Mountaineering Club (EVMC) is now over 50 years old, being formed on 13th December 1973 in the bottom bar of the Gloucester Arms (now Dockray Hall) in Penrith.
Based in the Eden Valley, members were very much involved in the development of crags and rock climbs in the Eden Valley in the 1970s, and continued explorations there and elsewhere in the Lake District and beyond. Members have extended their activities around the world on crags, fells and mountains on foot, skis, bikes, by kayak and even riding a unicycle. Through the Club, many lasting partnerships and close friendships have been formed.
The Club was instrumental in the building of the Eden Climbing Wall in Penrith in 1995 and has been closely involved with its operations since then.
Over the years there has been an interest in fell running. A number of members have completed the Bob Graham Round and in 1993 eight members traversed all the Wainwrights as a relay over 4 ½ days (see Chapter 11). In 2023 the Club members completed the Wainwrights without a Car which is detailed in this book.
The Club currently boasts an enthusiastic membership which covers a wide spread of interests, abilities and ages and more details are available on the club website - *www.evmc.co.uk*

Ron Kenyon
Founder Member and Club President 2024

ACKNOWLEDGEMENTS

The bringing together of this book has been an interesting experience and I hope it is well received. There have been a lot of people involved and I would like to thank all who have helped and in particular the following -

Robin Illingworth for coming up with the idea of *"Wainwrights without a car"*.

Members of the EVMC who participated in the ascents - Kevin Atherton, Gary Baum, Phil Blanshard, Al Davis, Jon Genesi, John Haworth, Dave Hellier, Chris Kenyon, Belinda Lloyd, Jane Meeks, Gary Newman, Eric Parker, Ian Phillips, Soo Redshaw, Mary Volume… as well as Tara, Rona, Barney and Skye.

Chris Sherwin for design, layout and illustrations on the inside of the cover

Don Sargeant for organising and drawing up the maps.

Gary Baum, Al Davis, Chris Kenyon and Ellie Sherwin for proofreading.

John Haworth for designing the Jagged Lakes logo

Leo Houlding, Rory Stewart, Steve Birkenshaw and Mark Richards for endorsing the book and their quotes.

Rob Hunter and Rick Salter for help with chapters on "Getting to know the area" and "Have a plan and come back safely" and quote by Rob as Chair (2024) of the Penrith Mountain Rescue Team.

The Wainwright Society for their support and quote.

Julian Cooper and Heaton-Cooper family for their agreement to include details of the concept of "best views of mountains".

Chris Beacock of Harvey Maps in relation to the chapter "Get to know the area".

Thanks to the Fix the Fells organisation for the work done on the fell path and also the piece included in this book, on that work.

Emma Moody, Lead Strategy Adviser, Recreation and Sustainable Transport, Lake District National Park Authority on ideas for and feedback on this book.

Mark Hodgkiss, Scheduled Bus Service office for Westmorland and Furness Council.

Stagecoach - thanks to Tom Waterhouse, Lauren Read, Ella van Thorpe and Richard Burgess for information on the 2025 bus routes and photographs of their buses and locations.

Warren Allison, secretary of the Cumbria Amenity Trust Mining History Society (CATMHS), in relation to information on mines.

Val Corbett for the photograph in Greenside Mines.

Alan Roper for copies and details of his paintings and sketches linked to meeting on Rannerdale Knotts.

Benni Fish for being at the right place and the right time when I wanted a photograph from the top of Castle Head.

Simon Curry for the photograph of the Lake District from 30,000 feet.

Wordsworth Trust for permission to use the image of the painting of Dove Cottage.

Cumberland and Westmorland Herald for hunting out and allowing use of the photograph of the Wainwright Relay Team.

I would also like to thank all the people we have met on the fells, as well as on the buses, trains and boats, over the year and for their stories and creac.

Jane Meeks and Rona looking for the next summit (walk **SE5**) - *Gary Baum*.

GENERAL INDEX

VALLEYS AND AREAS

Borrowdale & Keswick	25
Buttermere & Loweswater	23
Coniston	18
Duddon Valley	19
Ennerdale	22
Eskdale	19
Grasmere and Rydal	16
Great Langdale	17
Kentmere	14
Longsleddale	13
Mardale *(Haweswater)*	30
Newlands Valley	24
Penrith	29
Skiddaw Range	28
Thirlmere	27
Ullswater	29
Wasdale	20
Windermere	15

FELLS

Allan Crags	118		Crag Fell	152
Angletarn Crags	75		Crinkle Crags	122
Ard Crags	143		Dale Head	146
Armboth Fell	96		Dodd	107
Arnison Crag	54		Dollywaggon Pike	68
Arthur's Pike	74/ 83		Dove Crag	64
Bakestall	112		Dow Crag	128
Bannerdale Crags	106		Eagle Crag	95
Barf	139		Eel Crag	141
Barrow	138		Esk Pike	122
Base Brown	150		Fairfield	66
Beda Fell	82		Fellbarrow	155
Binsey	108		Fleetwith Pike	161
Birkhouse Moor	60		Froswick	84
Birks	66		Gavel Fell	156
Black Crag	128		Gibson Knott	99
Blake Fell	156		Glaramara	118
Blea Rigg	101		Glenridding Dodd	54
Bleaberry Fell	93		Gowbarrow Fell	61
Blencathra	113		Grange Fell	92
Bonscale Pike	83		Grasmoor	145
Bowfell	122		Gray Crag	79
Bowscale Fell	106		Graystones	139
Brae Fell	109		Great Borne	154
Brandreth	150		Great Calva	112
Branstree	79		Great Carrs	128
Brim Fell	128		Great Cockup	109
Brock Crags	75		Great Crag	92
Broom Fell	139		Great Dodd	60
Buckbarrow	152		Great End	126
Burnbank Fell	156		Great Gable	150
Calf Crag	99		Great Mell Fell	58
Carl Side	112		Great Rigg	67
Carrock Fell	113		Great Sca Fell	109
Castle Crag	136		Green Crag	119
Catbells	144		Green Gable	150
Catstycam	66		Grey Crag	79
Caudale Moor	81/ 85		Grey Friar	128
Causey Pike	141		Grey Knotts	150
Caw Fell	152		Grike	152
Clough Head	55/ 60		Grisedale Pike	145
Cold Pike	122		Hallin Fell	82
Coniston Old Man	128		Hard Knott	119

Harrison Stickle	99	Loft Crag	99	Seathwaite Fell	118
Hart Crag	64/ 66	Long Side	112	Selside Pike	79
Hart Side	69	Longlands Fell	109	Sergeant Man	99
Harter Fell *(Eskdale)*	119	Lonscale Fell	112	Sergeant's Crag	95
Harter Fell *(Mardale)*	79	Lord's Seat	139	Sheffield Pike	62
Hartsop Above How	64/ 66	Loughrigg Fell	95	Shipman Knotts	79
Hartsop Dodd	85	Low Fell	155	Silver How	95
Haycock	152	Low Pike	64	Skiddaw	112
Haystacks	151	Maiden Moor	144	Skiddaw Little Man	112
Helm Crag	99	Mardale Ill Bell	79	Slight Side	126
Helvellyn	60	Meal Fell	109	Sour Howes	84
Hen Comb	156	Mellbreak	156	Souther Fell	109
Heron Pike	67	Middle Dodd	65	St. Sunday Crag	66
High Crag	154	Middle Fell	152	Starling Dodd	154
High Hartsop Dodd	65	Mungrisdale Common	106	Steel Fell	99
High Pike *(Caldbeck)*	113	Nab Scar	67	Steel Knotts	84
High Pike *(Scandale)*	64	Nethermost Pike	68	Steeple	159
High Raise *(High Street)*	83	Outerside	138	Stone Arthur	67
High Raise *(Langstrath)*	99	Pavey Ark	99	Stybarrow Dodd	60
High Rigg	90	Pike o'Blisco	122	Swirl How	128
High Seat	91	Pike o'Stickle	99	Tarn Crag *(Easedale)*	98
High Spy	144	Pillar	159	Tarn Crag *(Longsleddale)*	79
High Stile	154	Place Fell	76	The Knott	81
High Street	81	Raise *(Helvellyn)*	60	The Nab	78
High Tove	96	Rampsgill Head	83	Thornthwaite Crag	79/ 81
Hindscarth	146	Rannerdale Knotts	141	Thunacar Knott	99
Holme Fell	128	Raven Crag	94	Troutbeck Tongue	84
Hopegill Head	145	Red Pike *(Buttermere)*	154	Ullock Pike	112
Ill Bell	84	Red Pike *(Wasdale)*	159	Ullscarf	96
Illgill Head	126	Red Screes	65	Walla Crag	93
Kentmere Pike	79	Rest Dodd	78	Wandope	141
Kidsty Pike	83	Robinson	146	Wansfell	77
Kirk Fell	159	Rossett Pike	122	Watson's Dodd	60
Knott	109	Rosthwaite Fell *(Bessyboot)*	118	Wether Hill	83
Knott Rigg	143	Sail	141	Wetherlam	128
Lank Rigg	152	Sale Fell	137/ 139	Whin Rigg	126
Latrigg	105	Sallows	84	Whinlatter	140
Ling Fell	137/ 139	Scafell	126	White Side	60
Lingmell	121	Scafell Pike	126	Whiteless Pike	141
Lingmoor Fell	122	Scar Crags	141	Whiteside	145
Little Hart Crag	65	Scoat Fell	159	Yewbarrow	162
Little Mell Fell	57	Seat Sandal	68	Yoke	84
Loadpot Hill	83	Seatallan	152		

THE BEGINNING AND THE END OF THE DAY

Above: Beginning of the day and the view from the best bus seat on the X4 to Keswick.

Below: Sunset on Ullswater, near Aira Force; a magical Lakeland moment.